HOT
Illustrations
FOR
Youth
Talks

4

Another 100
attention-getting tales,
narratives, & stories
with a message

Wayne Rice

Youth Specialties

ZONDERVAN

A DIVISION OF HARPERCOLLINS*PUBLISHERS*

D1401405

Hot Illustrations for Youth Talks 4: Another 100 attention-getting tales, narratives, and stories with a message

Copyright © 2001 by Wayne Rice

Youth Specialties books, 300 S. Pierce St., El Cajon, CA 92020, are published by Zondervan Publishing House, 5300 Patterson Ave. S.E., Grand Rapids, MI 49530.

Library of Congress Cataloging-in-Publication Data

Hot illustrations for youth talks 4 : another 100 attention-getting tales, narratives, and stories with a message / [complied by] Wayne Rice ; with contributions from many of America's top youth communicators, Les Christie ... [et al.].
    p. cm.
    Includes bibliographical references and index.
    ISBN 0-310-23619-3 (alk. paper)
    1. Homiletical illustrations. 2. Preaching to youth. I. Rice, Wayne. II. Christie, Les John.

BV4225.2 .H684 2001
251'.08—dc21

2001017558

The author and publisher acknowledge that some of the stories in this volume are of unknown origin, having been circulated orally or electronically, and without bylines or other identifying information. We've made every effort to track down the source of each story in this book. We apologize for any omissions.

We're grateful to the writers, publishers, and contributors of all the stories in this volume—and especially for the use of the following stories:

Prodigal Daughter (page 11): from *What's So Amazing About Grace?* by Philip Yancey. Copyright © 1997 by Philip D. Yancey. Used by permission of Zondervan Publishing House.

The Carpenter's Gift (page 70): first published as "The Perfect Mistake" in *Chicken Soup for the Christian Family Soul*, copyright © 2000 by Health Communications. Story reprinted by permission of Cheryl Walterman Stewart.

Oliver (page 117): from *The Power of the Powerless* by Christopher de Vinck. Copyright © 1998, 1995 by Christopher de Vinck. Used by permission of Zondervan Publishing House.

Can You Be Trusted? (page 170): from *Living Above the Level of Mediocrity* by Charles Swindoll. Copyright © 1990, Word Publishing, Nashville, Tennessee. All rights reserved. Used by permission.

Edited by Randy Southern
Interior illustrations by Joyce Revior
Cover and interior design by PAZ Design Group

Printed in the United States of America

01 02 03 04 05 06 07 / / 10 9 8 7 6 5 4 3 2 1

Contents

Alphabetical list of illustrations

Choosing and Using Illustrations

A young girl grows up on a cherry orchard just above Traverse City, Michigan. Her parents, a bit old-fashioned, tend to overreact to her nose ring, the music she listens to, and the length of her skirts. They ground her a few times and she seethes inside. "I hate you!" she screams at her father when he knocks on the door of her room after an argument, and that night she acts on a plan she has mentally rehearsed scores of times. She runs away.

She has visited Detroit only once before, on a bus trip with her church youth group to watch the Tigers play. Because newspapers in Traverse City report in lurid detail the gangs, the drugs, and the violence in downtown Detroit, she concludes that is probably the last place her parents will look for her. California, maybe, or Florida, but not Detroit.

Her second day there she meets a man who drives the biggest car she's ever seen. He offers her a ride, buys her lunch, arranges a place for her to stay. He gives her some pills that make her feel better than she's ever felt before. She was right all along, she decides: her parents were keeping her from all the fun.

The good life continues for a month, two months, a year. The man with the big car—she calls him "Boss"—teaches her a few things that men like. Since she's underage, men pay a premium for her. She lives in a penthouse and orders room service whenever she wants. Occasionally she thinks about the folks back home, but their lives now seem so boring and provincial that she can hardly believe she grew up there.

She has a brief scare when she sees her picture printed on the back of a milk carton with the headline "Have you seen this child?" But by now she has blond hair, and with all the makeup and body-piercing jewelry she wears, nobody would mistake her for a child. Besides, most of her friends are runaways, and nobody squeals in Detroit.

After a year the first sallow signs of illness appears, and it amazes her how fast the boss turns mean. "These days, we can't mess around," he growls, and before she knows it she's out on the street without a penny to her name. She still turns a couple of tricks a night, but they don't pay much and all the money goes to support her habit. When winter blows in she finds herself sleeping on metal grates outside the big department stores. "Sleeping" is the wrong word—a teenage girl at night in downtown Detroit can never relax her guard. Dark bands circle her eyes. Her cough worsens.

One night as she lies awake listening for footsteps, all of a sudden everything about her life looks different. She no longer feels like a woman of the world. She feels like a little girl, lost in a cold and frightening city. She begins to whimper. Her pockets are empty and she's hungry. She needs a fix. She pulls her legs tight underneath her and shivers under the newspapers she's piled atop her coat. Something jolts a synapse of memory and a single image fills her mind: of May in Traverse City, when a million cherry trees bloom at once, with her golden retriever dashing through the rows and rows of blossomy trees in chase of a tennis ball.

God, why did I leave, she says to herself, and pain stabs at her heart. My dog back home eats better than I do now. She's sobbing, and she knows in a flash that more than anything else in the world, she wants to go home.

Three straight phone calls, three straight connections with the answering machine. She hangs up without leaving a message the first two times, but the third time she says, "Dad, Mom, it's me. I was wondering about maybe coming home. I'm catching a bus up your way, and it'll get there about midnight tomorrow. If you're not there, well, I guess I'll just stay on the bus until it hits Canada."

It takes about seven hours for a bus to make all the stops between Detroit and Traverse City, and during that time she realizes the flaws in her plan. What if her parents are out of town and miss the message? Shouldn't she have waited another day or so until she could talk to them? And even if they are home, they probably wrote her off as dead long ago. She should have given them some time to overcome the shock.

Her thoughts bounce back and forth between those worries and the speech she is preparing for her father. "Dad, I'm sorry. I know I was wrong. It's not your fault; it's all mine. Dad, can you forgive me?" She says the words over and over, her throat tightening even as she rehearses them. She hasn't apologized to anyone in years.

The bus has been driving with lights on since Bay City. Tiny snowflakes hit the pavement rubbed worn by thousands of tires, and the asphalt steams. She's forgotten how dark it gets at night out here. A deer darts across the road and the bus swerves. Every so often, a billboard. A sign posting the mileage to Traverse City. Oh, God.

When the bus finally rolls into the station, its air brakes hissing in protest, the driver announces in a crackly voice over the microphone, "Fifteen minutes, folks. That's all we have here." Fifteen minutes to decide her life. She checks herself in a compact mirror, smooths her hair, and licks the lipstick off her teeth. She looks at the tobacco stains on her fingertips and wonders if her parents will notice. If they're here.

She walks into the terminal not knowing what to expect. Not one of the thousand scenes that have played out in her mind prepares her for what she sees. There, in the concrete-walls-and-plastic-chairs bus terminal in Traverse City, Michigan, stands a group of forty brothers and sisters and great aunts and uncles and cousins and grandmother and great-grandmother to boot. They're all wearing goofy party hats and blowing noisemakers, and taped across the entire wall of the terminal is a computer-generated banner that reads "Welcome home!"

Out of the crowd of well-wishers breaks her Dad. She stares out through the tears quivering in her eyes like hot mercury and begins the memorized speech, "Dad, I'm sorry. I know..."

He interrupts her. "Hush, child. We've got no time for that. No time for apologies. You'll be late for the party. A banquet's waiting for you at home."

Sound familiar? The story was written by Philip Yancey (from his book *What's So Amazing About Grace?*), but the plot came from the Master Storyteller, Jesus of Nazareth (Luke 15:11-32).

Jesus appreciated the power of a good anecdote. In fact, Scripture records that Jesus never spoke without using a parable (Matthew 13:34). He consistently sprinkled his teaching with stories and real-life situations to drive home his points. He drew his illustrations from everyday life in the Middle East, describing farmers and families, sheep and goats, barns and wheat fields—and people were "amazed" at his teaching (Matthew 7:28).

Amazing is not how most teenagers describe church speakers and

teachers. Boring is probably a more accurate description. A few speakers, however, know how to capture the attention of kids and communicate well with them. Invariably these speakers use stories in their talks.

This book, like the others in the Hot Illustrations series, is a selected compilation of 100 stories that speakers have used effectively in youth talks. I have used many of them myself. All of them will work with kids if the stories are chosen with care and communicated with conviction and purpose.

Adults will enjoy them as well. In fact, I think we're wrong to assume that adults prefer dull and boring abstractions to interesting and colorful illustrations. I find that the best way to communicate with adults is to speak to them as if they're all about 14 years old. (That assumes, of course, that you don't speak to 14-year-olds like they're children.)

Keep in mind that this is not an exhaustive collection of illustrations. Those books which claim to be exhaustive are often too large and difficult to use. I have one book on my shelf boasting of nearly 8,000 anecdotes. But to be honest, it's hard for me to find one good illustration in that book when I need it. My goal for the Hot Illustrations series has been to offer you quality illustrations rather than quantity.

Since selecting and using stories is a very subjective and personal exercise, what works for you may not work for me (and vice versa). Nevertheless, this book offers you a good sampling of illustrations I can recommend without reservation. Much of my confidence has to do with the quality people who contributed to this book (whose names you'll find on page 190), and I thank all of them for sharing their material with us. I know the value of good anecdotes—they're hard to come by. Many speakers prefer keeping their stories to themselves. We who do regular public speaking are indebted to all those who contributed to this book.

Choose the concrete, the interesting, and the unpredictable.

An effective story uses concrete images—familiar to the hearer and drawn from everyday life. Even the most illiterate, uneducated peasant could identify with the situations, objects, and people Jesus described in his parables. One reason the old hymn "Amazing Grace" has remained popular over the years is because of its familiar, concrete language:

Amazing grace, how sweet the sound, that saved a wretch like me. I once was lost, but now I'm found, was blind but now I see.

Contrast those stirring words with the following version:

Unexpected lenience, in the form of a mellifluous tonality, preserved an organism of questionable value commonly associated with the author of this composition. Said ego was one time misplaced, but the situation has been altered, and currently, there is no doubt as to its location. In addition, said ego formerly was incapacitated by a malfunction of the visual sense, but at this moment has recovered the associated ability.

If you think this rendition is hard to understand, try singing it.

Along with using concrete images, a good illustration is interesting. A story needs a plot that engages the listener all the way to its conclusion. Take, for example, the parables Jesus told. People caught up in his stories lowered their defenses, allowing Jesus to drop a truth bomb on them.

Finally, and perhaps most importantly, an effective illustration uses surprise. The unpredictable climax is what makes a joke funny, a movie suspenseful, and an anecdote powerful. Surprise helps drive a message home. Surprises are remembered. More than once Jesus' illustrations captivated listeners who were comfortable in their certainty that the point was meant for some other group of people. Then, watch out! The ending pointed the finger at themselves.

The Old Testament prophet Nathan used the element of surprise to change King David's opinion about his adultery and murder. When David heard Nathan's story of the rich man with many sheep who confiscated from the poor man his one pet lamb, David became incensed (2 Samuel 12). He angrily demanded that the evil rich man be brought to justice. What a surprise when Nathan enlightened David that he had just pronounced judgment on himself.

Start by choosing the point of your talk, not by finding a riveting illustration.

Illustrations are not the points you're attempting to communicate.

Don't build your talk around a story you're eager to use. Decide the truth you want to make known, and then find or create an illustration that will breathe life into it.

A young boy received a bow and arrow from his father and immediately went outside to try it out. Checking on his boy a few minutes later, the father was amazed to see that the boy had hit the bull's-eye in several targets crudely drawn on the side of a fence. Impressed by his son's achievement, he said to his son, "I didn't realize you were such a good shot!"

"Oh, it was easy," the boy replied. "I shot the arrows first, then drew the targets around them."

Creating a talk around an illustration is like drawing targets around your arrows. First draw your target—decide what truth you desire to communicate. Once you know where your arrow needs to end up, speed it on its way with a fitting anecdote.

To help you match your talk with an anecdote, consult the topical listing on page 6. Also, each story in this book is followed with a suggestion or two about "where to take it from here." However, since every story has an unlimited number of applications, my recommendations are only the most obvious applications.

When your point is obvious, don't illustrate it.

Suppose I stood up in front of a group and said, "God is good." The truth of that claim may not be clear to some people. I probably need to illustrate it with a story, example, or analogy that describes what I mean. If, however, your group was meeting in a room registering 40 degrees on the thermostat and I said, "This room is cold," then an illustration would belabor the point. My audience doesn't need to be enlightened by a story about someone freezing to death.

Limit the number of illustrations you use in one talk.

One good anecdote per point is usually plenty. Listeners are influenced for a longer time by a single illustration than by a point that's cluttered with several stories. If your friend tells you one joke, for example, you'll probably tell it yourself to a few other friends. But if your friend tells you two jokes, by the time you're through laughing at the second joke, you'll likely have already forgotten the first one.

A seminar speaker I heard recently must have used 20 or more stories one evening. The audience laughed throughout the session. Yet in spite of the quality illustrations, I found it difficult afterward to remember any of them, not to mention the point of any of them. Make your point and illustrate it well, then move on to another point—or just stop. Piling illustration upon illustration is like continuing to hammer a nail once the nail is in all the way—after that, all the hammer does is batter the wood.

Leave your audience room to think for themselves.

An audience can feel put off if you pre-chew a point and attempt to serve it up to them with an explicit application. At times it's appropriate to make sure that the audience gets the point quickly by explaining it in detail. Jesus explained to his close disciples the meaning of the symbols in the parable of the sower, for instance. But most of the time, Jesus simply told a story and then allowed his audience to think about it for a while and to discuss its meaning among themselves. Sometimes the listeners came to different conclusions. That's okay.

When Jesus' disciples asked him why he used parables, he explained that parables allowed those with an open heart to hear what God wanted them to hear (Matthew 13:10-17). But those with "hardened hearts" were kept in the dark. Jesus stimulated his disciples to learn by allowing them to ponder on their own the meaning of his parables (Matthew 13:36). And of course, we are also the beneficiaries of this strategy of the Master Teacher.

Use illustrations to recapture the audience's attention.

I'm always amazed at how an audience can be dozing off, doodling on program covers, whispering to each other—and then the speaker starts telling a story. On cue, everyone's head raises and every eye turns to the speaker. Unfortunately, what usually follows that magic moment of undivided attention is the end of the story—at which time everyone goes back to what they were doing.

A good speaker avoids this disheartening experience by making his application as poignant (without using the word poignant) and interesting as the story itself. That's why I warned you earlier to build your talk first and then select your illustration. A properly chosen story merely wets the appetite of the audience—they'll stay tuned to discover what your point is.

Change the pace in your talk by using illustrations.

When you're ready to shift gears in a talk, you may select an illustration for no other reason than to set up the audience for the point you're moving toward. In other words, the illustration may not communicate the truth you have in mind, but its humor serves as an ice breaker, its surprise opens the door on a new topic, its sentiment softens a challenge so the listeners stay with you to your conclusion.

Jokes, of course, are useful pace changers. I've used jokes—and there are many in this book—for no other reason than to build a bridge to a more serious point that I want to make. Sometimes the application is thin at best, but it works—as long as it's not overdone.

An effective speaker makes every part of his or her talk do meaningful work. Although illustrations may be used merely to hold a group's attention or to get laughs, if those are their only purposes, the audience will become frustrated and bored. Like the boy who cried, "Wolf!" when there was no wolf, the audience eventually tires of a speaker who has no content to his message.

I attended a function a few years ago that featured a well-known speaker, popular on the banquet circuit. He used dozens of jokes, stories, and illustrations—some of them very entertaining. But his disjointed talk never went anywhere. He had no point to make—or if he did, he never developed it in such a way that the audience could remember what it was. In spite of the continuing laughter that greeted the speaker's funny stories, after an hour I could tell that the audience had had enough. They wanted to go home. Speakers who are light on content and heavy on entertainment are often insecure people whose primary concern is not to communicate a message, but to make the audience like them. That's okay if you're a standup comic, but not if you're entrusted with the life-changing message of the gospel.

Choose illustrations you can tell with authenticity.

Some of the illustrations in this book need to be communicated with a dramatic flair or with casual humor. If telling a joke makes you tense or if your most dramatic moment was placing an exclamation mark in a letter to your church's director of Christian education, you may want to avoid telling a story that requires a flair for humor—or at least save it for when you loosen up.

As you consider whether to use a particular illustration, ask yourself, "How comfortable will I feel using this one? Is this me?" I remember trying to do Bill Cosby impressions when I was younger—and making a complete fool of myself. I couldn't understand why it was so funny when Bill Cosby did it and a bomb when I used the same routines. I know now. It's because I'm stuck with being me, not Bill Cosby. Since discovering that truth, when I speak I limit my illustrations to those that I can communicate with credibility and conviction.

Once you select a story from among the many in this book that fit your style, rehearse until you can present it convincingly. Memorize it if necessary. There's nothing worse than launching into an illustration only to realize halfway through that you can't remember the part that made the illustration work. It's hard to go back and salvage the point. Believe me, I know.

Some of the stories in this book are meant to be read to the audience. If you're in the early experimental stages of using illustrations, try these first. Just photocopy the appropriate page and tuck it into your Bible or lesson book. Don't read directly from this book.

Choose illustrations with your audience in mind.

Not all illustrations are appropriate for every audience. The anecdotes in this book were selected primarily because they are, generally speak-

ing, effective with adolescents. That doesn't mean they deal only with adolescent concerns. It just means that adolescents are the group that will best relate to the stories and get the point if you communicate it well.

Most of the illustrations in this book are stories, as opposed to quotes or statistics. That's because adolescents love stories—particularly stories that teach a lesson. Teenagers enjoy the often new experience of making connections between concrete illustrations and abstract ideas.

Make a distinction between true stories and stories that communicate truth.

Most anecdotes aren't entirely true to begin with—even those that happen to you. I'll tell you right up front that none of the illustrations in this book are true. Some of them are based on historical events, but they are presented here as illustrations, not history. In the telling and retelling of these anecdotes, they've been altered and embellished to make them effective illustrations. At best, they're only partially true. Tony Campolo likes to wink and say about some of his anecdotes, "Well, if it didn't happen that way, it should have."

Illustrations, including the ones offered in this book and most of the stories that Jesus told, are nothing more than stories or parables that communicate truth. Parables are, by definition, fictional. Jesus made up his parables. There never was an actual Prodigal Son, as far as we know. Jesus invented the story to illustrate a point and did it so well that it has become one of the most beloved stories of all time.

Personalize your illustrations.

Enliven anecdotes by adding color to them, changing the details, renaming the characters, and generally tailoring them to your audience—especially when you're telling a story from the Bible. Kids listen better when they can relate the story to familiar people, places, and events. Your kids may find it easier to relate to a runaway teenage girl in Detroit than to the Prodigal Son of Jesus' time.

Although personalizing illustrations enhances their effectiveness, don't lie to make yourself look important, look good, or even look bad. Be honest with your audience; you'll not only be more effective, but you'll have nothing that can come back later to haunt you.

You can personalize stories by relating them to something that actually happened to you, but don't lie. A well-known Christian youth speaker recently lost his entire ministry when it was discovered that much of what he had claimed to be true over the years was actually false. No talk is important enough to lie for. Anything short of the truth is unethical and has no place in the ministry of the church.

Credit the source of the illustrations you use.

Telling someone else's story as if it happened to you or as if you thought of it is a form of plagiarism, in most cases. I know several speakers who can hardly use their own talks anymore because other people have "stolen" their illustrations and examples and made them their own. Tony Campolo laughs about the time he was about to deliver his famous "It's Friday, but Sunday's Comin'" message to a church. The pastor urged him not to "because my congregation thinks that story happened to me."

The best way to use an illustration associated with someone else is to simply credit the source. If that pastor had only said "Tony Campolo tells a wonderful story about the time he..." Of course, that disclaimer might lessen the effectiveness of the illustration— in which case it may not be the best one to use at all.

This book contains few illustrations personal to an individual speaker. That kind is difficult to transfer to you or to tell in the third person. I've compiled only those anecdotes that anyone can use.

Good illustrations also show up in your own life experiences and in the life experiences of others you know. Powerful illustrations can be derived from television, the movies, books, magazines, and newspapers. Keep your eyes and ears open, and file your discoveries for future use.

In short, your goal is the accurate communication of the truth, so that what you say matches what your students hear, understand, and apply. I trust this book will help you achieve that goal next time you stand in front of an adolescent audience.

Pull, Buddy!

A man from the big city was enjoying a relaxing drive in the country when a dog ran in front of his car. He swerved to miss it but lost control of his car and ended up in a ditch. After a few unsuccessful attempts to get his car out, the man sat on his bumper and waited for help to arrive.

He didn't have to wait long. A farmer who lived just down the road came to his aid with a big, powerful-looking horse.

The man watched as the farmer hitched the horse to the car's bumper. When the rope was secure, the farmer yelled, "Pull, Nellie, pull!" But the horse didn't move.

Then the farmer yelled, "Pull, Buster, pull!" But the horse didn't move.

Next the farmer yelled, "Pull, Coco, pull!" But the horse still didn't move.

Finally, the farmer said, "Pull, Buddy, pull!" And the horse dragged the car from the ditch with very little effort.

The motorist was appreciative—and a little curious. "Why did you call out four names when your horse only responded to one?" he asked.

The farmer smiled. "Oh, Buddy is blind," he explained, "and if he thought he was the only one pulling he wouldn't even try!"

 WHERE TO TAKE IT FROM HERE...

Just like Buddy, we need other people to bring out the best in us. As the Scripture says, "Though one may be overpowered, two can defend themselves. A cord of three strands is not quickly broken" (Ecclesiastes 4:12). That's why God created us to be part of a community, part of a family, part of the church.

It's very difficult to live the Christian life alone. It can be done, but like the verse says, one can be overpowered. The devil will find you easy prey. When you have others who are standing with you—even though they are not physically present—you can draw strength and encouragement from their prayers and support. We all really need each other.

The House in the Dark

The O'Learys and the MacMillans lived as neighbors at the turn of the century. One day a young man in a suit came to their village to explain that they would soon have electricity for the first time. The MacMillans responded with their typical enthusiasm and filled out the appropriate papers to have their house wired.

The O'Learys were more cautious. After all, they had lived for generations without electricity and had managed just fine. They weren't about to throw money after every passing fad. So they decided to wait. If electricity was as good as everyone said, they could always sign up later.

In the weeks that followed, the MacMillans busily prepared their house for electrical power. They clamped wires and sockets to the walls and hung bulbs from the ceiling.

When the big day finally came, the MacMillans invited their neighbors, including the O'Learys, to a grand lighting party. With a dramatic flourish, Mr. MacMillan threw a switch and the bulbs began to glow for the first time. The MacMillan house was illuminated more brightly than it had ever been lit before.

There was a gasp. "How lovely!" someone said.

Then another gasp. "How filthy!" someone else said.

It was true. No one had noticed it before in the dim light, but years of oil lamps had left a film of dingy soot over everything. The walls were grimy, there were cobwebs in the corner, and dust covered the floor.

The O'Learys decided right then and there that they would never install electricity in their home. They would never suffer the humiliation of having their dirty home exposed by the light.

After the party, the MacMillans went to work. They scrubbed the soot off the walls and ceiling, cleaned the cobwebs, and swept away the dust. They had indeed been embarrassed by their dirty home when the lights came on, but within a day, their house was cleaner than it had ever been.

Meanwhile, the O'Learys continued to live comfortably in their dimly lit home filled with soot, cobwebs, and filth.

? WHERE TO TAKE IT FROM HERE...

Many people today choose to live in the dark. They don't want anyone to see the dirt—what's really going on in their lives. Sometimes they don't want to see it themselves. They avoid the light for fear that they will see the truth and be forced to clean up their acts.

"This is the verdict: Light has come into the world, but men loved darkness instead of light because their deeds were evil. Everyone who does evil hates the light, and will not come into the light for fear that his deeds will be exposed. But whoever lives by the truth comes into the light, so that it may be seen plainly that what he has done has been done through God" (John 3:19-21).

CAR JACKING FOILED!

Not long ago in California, an elderly woman went to the grocery store to do some shopping. When she returned to her car, she noticed four men getting into it.

The woman dropped her shopping bags, reached into her purse, and pulled out a small handgun that she carried for protection. She ran to the front of her car, aimed the pistol at the men, and began screaming at them at the top of her lungs. She ordered them out of the car and warned that if they didn't, she would blow their brains out.

"I know how to use this gun, and don't think I won't!" she screamed.

The four men didn't hesitate. The threw open the car doors, scrambled out, and started running as fast as they could.

The woman was trembling, but kept her composure. When she was certain the men were gone, she put the gun back in her purse, picked up her bags, and loaded them into the back seat of the car. She then climbed into the driver's seat and decided to go immediately to the police station to report the incident.

But there was a small problem. Her key wouldn't fit in the ignition. A quick glance around the interior confirmed that she was in the wrong car! Her vehicle was parked four spaces away in the same aisle of the parking lot.

She loaded her bags into her own car and drove to the police station to confess what she had done. When she told the story to the sergeant, he couldn't control his laughter. He just pointed to the other end of the counter where four very shaken men were reporting a car jacking by a mad, elderly white woman.

The woman apologized, and no charges were filed.

Things are not always as they first appear, are they? Have you ever jumped to conclusions about someone only to later find out that you were badly mistaken? You may not have pulled a gun, but you may have hurt someone with unkind words or gestures. You may have spread a rumor that wasn't true or refused to include someone in your circle of friends.

Like the woman in the parking lot, many of us have a tendency to assume the worst about people. We don't think; we just "know" that we are right and they are wrong. Until we find out otherwise.

Jesus taught his disciples to avoid judging others or accusing them false-ly (see Matthew 7:1; John 7:24). If you follow that example, you won't have to worry about being embarrassed or having to apologize later.

FARMER FLEMING

A poor Scottish farmer by the name of Fleming was working in his field one day when he heard a cry coming from a nearby bog. Immediately he dropped his tools and rushed toward the sound of the cries.

When he got to the bog, he saw a terrified young boy trying to fight his way out of the thick black muck, with very little success. Farmer Fleming waded into the bog, grabbed the young boy, and saved him from what would have been a slow and painful death.

The next day, a fancy carriage pulled up to the Fleming's small, rundown farmhouse. An elegantly dressed nobleman stepped out and introduced himself as the father of the boy Farmer Fleming had saved.

"I want to repay you" said the nobleman. "You saved my son's life."

"No, I can't accept payment for what I did," Fleming replied. At that moment, a young boy came to the door of the farmhouse.

"Is that your son?" the nobleman asked.

"Yes," replied the farmer.

"I have a proposition for you," the nobleman continued. "Let me take your son with me and give him a good education. If the lad is anything

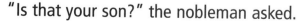

like his father, he will grow to be a man you can be proud of."

Knowing what an expensive education could mean for his son, Farmer Fleming accepted the offer. In time, his son graduated from St. Mary's Hospital Medical School in London and became known throughout the world as Sir Alexander Fleming, the discoverer of penicillin.

But that's not the end of the story. Years later, the nobleman's son was stricken with pneumonia. His life was saved by...penicillin.

The nobleman's name was Lord Randolf Churchill. His son's name was Winston.

Yes, *that* Winston Churchill.

 **WHERE TO TAKE IT FROM HERE...**

Do you ever wonder if what you do makes any real difference to anyone? History has proven over and over that God uses seemingly insignificant actions to change lives and impact the world in ways we may never realize. Nothing we do for God is insignificant. "Give, and it will be given to you. A good measure, pressed down, shaken together and running over, will be poured into your lap (Luke 6:38).

Dead or Alive?

Two brothers were arguing about the wisdom of their parents. "Father is very wise," said the first brother. "We should listen to him and do what he says."

The second brother disagreed. "Father is not so wise! Why, we are just as smart as he is. I'll prove it to you!"

The next day the second brother went into the woods near his home and captured a small bird. He brought the bird home and said to his brother, "Let's go find our father. I will show you that he isn't so smart!"

The two brothers went into their father's study, the second one holding the small bird between his cupped hands. "Father, I have a question for you," he said. "I hold a small bird in my hands. Tell me, is this bird dead or alive?"

The boy was confident that his father would not answer correctly because if he said that the bird was dead, the boy would simply open his hands and show that the bird was alive. If his father answered that the bird was alive, he would crush the bird between his hands and reveal that the bird was dead. Then he would prove to his brother that his father was not so wise after all.

The boys' father considered the question for a moment and said, "My son...the answer is in your hands."

 WHERE TO TAKE IT FROM HERE...

Sometimes we come to our Heavenly Father with questions that are just as impossible to answer. "Tell me, God, what should I do with my life? Who should I marry? Where should I live? What will my future hold?" We expect God to arrange our lives for us and make everything work out just right. After all, isn't that what an all-powerful, all-knowing God is for?

The answer is no. In his wisdom, God created us with free will. In effect, He says to us, "My son, my daughter, the answer is in your hands."

While God does know the future—and most certainly has the power to determine it—he has graciously given us control over our own lives. He created us in his own image; that is, with the ability to choose, to decide what we will do, how we will live, whom we will serve.

He chose not be a cosmic puppeteer, simply pulling the strings of our lives and making us into people who would automatically serve him and love him. Instead, he gave us the ability to decide for ourselves whether to love him or not, whether to obey him or not, and whether to serve him or not. He wants us to have eternal life (see 2 Peter 3:9), but the "answer is in our hands" (see Deuteronomy 30:19 and Joshua 24:15).

The Egg Toss

During the waning days of World War II, thousands of Russian troops poured into the city of Berlin. Many of them were simple country bumpkins who had never been in a city before. They were amazed and confused by what they saw. Some soldiers unscrewed light bulbs and carefully packed them away to take home, believing they contained light and could be made to work anywhere.

One group of Russian soldiers burst into a Berlin chemical lab. Ransacking the offices and laboratories, they came upon a dozen eggs sealed in an airtight container, emblazoned with bright red German words.

Like kids at a picnic, the soldiers put down their weapons, pulled off their heavy overcoats, and began playing an old-fashioned egg toss. Just then a lab scientist stumbled upon the scene. Horrified, he started shouting at the soldiers. But since the Russians could not understand German, they ignored him and continued their game.

Finally the scientist found a Russian colonel who could translate. The colonel ordered the soldiers to carefully replace the eggs in their containers and get out of the building, which was then locked up tight.

What the soldiers didn't realize was that the eggs they were playing with so nonchalantly contained the deadly typhus virus. If even one of them had broken, the soldiers would have certainly died and infected the entire population.

 WHERE TO TAKE IT FROM HERE...

Many people play around with sin as if it were some kind of game. And though it may look harmless—even innocent—to them, they are, in fact, playing with death.

That's why the Bible is so emphatic about the consequences of sin. God isn't trying to squelch our fun; instead, he wants us to live life to its fullest. "For the wages of sin is death, but the gift of God is eternal life in Jesus Christ our Lord" (Romans 6:23).

Remember that Satan always tries to deceive us (2 Corinthians 11:3) by making sin look harmless, exciting, and fun. Don't be misled. You may not be as lucky as those soldiers.

The People Who Brought You this Book...

invite you to discover MORE valuable youth ministry resources.

Youth Specialities has three decades of experience working alongside Christian youth workers of just about every denomination and youth-serving organization. We're here to help you, whether you're brand new to youth ministry or a veteran, whether you're a volunteer or a career youth pastor. Each year we serve over 100,000 youth workers worldwide through our training seminars, conventions, magazines, resource products, and internet Web site (www.YouthSpecialties.com).

For FREE information about ways YS can help your youth ministry, complete and return this card.

Are you: ☐ A paid youth worker   ☐ A volunteer   S=480001

Name_____

Church/Org. _____

Address ☐ Church or ☐ Home _____

City _____State _____Zip _____

Daytime Phone Number (_____) _____

E-Mail _____

Denomination _____ Average Weekly Church Attendance _____

The People Who Brought You this Book...

invite you to discover MORE valuable youth ministry resources.

Youth Specialities has three decades of experience working alongside Christian youth workers of just about every denomination and youth-serving organization. We're here to help you, whether you're brand new to youth ministry or a veteran, whether you're a volunteer or a career youth pastor. Each year we serve over 100,000 youth workers worldwide through our training seminars, conventions, magazines, resource products, and internet Web site (www.YouthSpecialties.com).

For FREE information about ways YS can help your youth ministry, complete and return this card.

Are you: ☐ A paid youth worker   ☐ A volunteer   S=480001

Name_____

Church/Org. _____

Address ☐ Church or ☐ Home _____

City _____State _____Zip _____

Daytime Phone Number (_____) _____

E-Mail _____

Denomination _____ Average Weekly Church Attendance _____

BUSINESS REPLY MAIL

FIRST-CLASS MAIL   PERMIT 268   HOLMES PA

POSTAGE WILL BE PAID BY ADDRESSEE

YOUTH SPECIALTIES
P.O. BOX 668
HOLMES, PA 19043-0668

NO POSTAGE
NECESSARY
IF MAILED
IN THE
UNITED STATES

BUSINESS REPLY MAIL

FIRST-CLASS MAIL   PERMIT 268   HOLMES PA

POSTAGE WILL BE PAID BY ADDRESSEE

YOUTH SPECIALTIES
P.O. BOX 668
HOLMES, PA 19043-0668

Bad Tire, Good Business

An elderly woman walked into a large department store and approached a salesperson. She explained that she wanted to return an automobile tire she felt was unsuitable for her car. The salesperson discovered that she had been a longtime customer of his store and that she and her friends spent much of their time there.

But, she said, she was unhappy with the tire she had purchased. The salesperson was surprised, but asked if she had the tire with her. She told him she had the tire in her car, but that she had lost the receipt.

"Well, that's not a problem," the salesperson said after a moment of thought. "You can return the tire. Would a store credit be okay?"

The woman agreed and the salesperson gave her a store voucher for the full value of the tire.

You may think there's nothing extraordinary about how this particular salesperson handled the situation. After all, he worked it out so that the woman would still end up spending her money in his department store. And she would probably tell her friends how fairly and respectfully she was treated there. So it was just good business, right?

Well, yes. But there's something else you should know. This incident occurred in a store that doesn't sell automotive equipment—not even tires.

? WHERE TO TAKE IT FROM HERE...

This is the kind of story that Jesus might have told. Consider the parable of the laborers in the vineyard who were paid a full day's wage even though they worked only an hour or two (Matthew 20:1-16). Or the story of the prodigal son, who received a gala homecoming party even though he had been selfish and rebellious (Luke 15:11-32). Those are grace stories—stories about people who received good things they didn't deserve.

Sometimes you may want to believe that if you're good enough, you can earn your way to heaven and eternal life. On the other hand, you may worry that God will never let you into heaven because you've been so bad.

But that's not how grace works. Grace is not about what you've done in the past or about what you can do in the future. It's about what God can do right now.

Just as the store salesperson gave the elderly woman store credit because he could, so God credits us with eternal life because he can. He loves us and will do anything he can to make it possible for us to draw near to him. "For God so loved the world that he gave his one and only Son, that whoever believes in him shall not perish but have eternal life" (John 3:16). "But God demonstrates his own love for us in this: While we were still sinners, Christ died for us" (Romans 5:8).

And now Jesus calls us to treat others with grace as well. Hey, if a department store can do it, so can you.

34

The Stonecutter

Once upon a time, there lived a stonecutter who went every day to the mountain to cut stones. And while he worked he whistled and sang, for though he was poor, he had everything he wanted. He was a happy man.

Then one day he was called to work at the mansion of a very rich man. When he saw the man's beautiful house, the stonecutter felt a pang of desire for the first time in his life. He said, "If only I were rich, I would not have to earn my living with hard work and sweat."

Suddenly a voice from heaven boomed, "Your wish is granted. From now on, anything you want will be given to you."

When the stonecutter returned home that evening, to his amazement, he found a mansion in place of his small hut!

The stonecutter gave up cutting stones and began to live the life of the rich. One day he was sitting in front of his mansion when he saw a king and all of his noblemen passing by. He said to himself; "I wish I were a king, sitting in the cool comfort of a royal carriage."

No sooner had he made his wish than he found himself riding in a cool, comfortable carriage, dressed in royal garb and surrounded by servants.

As the journey continued, the day got warmer and the interior of the carriage became unbearably hot. The stonecutter/king looked out the carriage window and marveled at the power of the sun. He said to himself, "I wish I were the sun."

Once again his wish was granted and he became the sun, sending out waves of heat to the entire universe.

All went well for a while. Then one rainy day, the stonecutter/king/sun tried to make his heat penetrate a thick bank of clouds. But he couldn't do it. The clouds were too dense. The people below the clouds could not feel his heat.

"I wish I were a cloud," he said. And that's what he became. As a cloud, he enjoyed his power to prevent the sun's heat from reaching the ground.

Soon, though, the stonecutter/king/sun/cloud felt himself being pushed by a great force. He realized that the force was the wind and that he was no match for it. "I wish I were the wind," he said. And that's what he became. As the mighty wind, he blew clouds and rain all over the kingdom. Sometimes he even blew down trees and buildings with the strength of a hurricane.

But it wasn't long, though, before the stonecutter/king/sun/cloud/wind found something that he could not move by blowing. It was a huge, towering stone, glorious in its sheer size, weight, and strength. No matter how hard he tried, he just couldn't move that stone.

"I wish I were that stone," he said. In an instant, he became the stone, stronger than anything on earth.

But while he stood there in all of his stony glory, he heard the sound of a hammer and chisel pounding into solid rock. He looked down and saw a stonecutter cutting chunks of rock from his feet.

And the stonecutter/king/sun/cloud/wind/stone said, "How can a tiny creature like that be more powerful than a mighty rock like me? I want to be a man!"

The stonecutter was instantly transformed into a man again.

And today he can still be found going up to the mountain to cut stone, singing and whistling all the way.

WHERE TO TAKE IT FROM HERE...

Though this Jewish parable is centuries old, it carries a timeless message. Have you ever wished you were somebody else? Have you ever wanted what someone else had?

God wants us to be content with who we are and what we have right now. When you can't be content with your present, you probably won't be content with your future. You'll always want more.

Paul wrote, "I have learned the secret of being content in any and every situation, whether well fed or hungry, whether living in plenty or in want" (Philippians 4:12). The secret to contentment is being aware of the fact that God knows your needs and will always take care of you. He is a giver of good and perfect gifts (James 1:17).

"Keep your lives free from the love of money and be content with what you have, because God has said, 'Never will I leave you; never will I forsake you'" (Hebrews 13:5). He is all you need.

Real Pearls

The cheerful girl with bouncy curls was almost five. Waiting with her mother at the checkout stand, she saw a circle of glistening white pearls in a pink foil box. "Oh please, Mommy. Can I have them? Please, Mommy, please?"

Her mother checked the back of the little foil box and said, "Jenny, these pearls cost $1.95. If you really want them, I'll think of some extra chores for you to do and raise your allowance. It won't take long for you to save enough money to buy them yourself."

Her mother was right. After only two weeks, Jenny had enough money saved for the pearls. Her mother took her back to the store, where Jenny proudly counted out her money to the cashier.

Jenny loved her pearls. They made her feel pretty and grown up. She wore them everywhere—Sunday school, kindergarten, even to bed. The only time she took them off was when she went swimming or took a bubble bath. Her mother said that if they got wet, they might turn her neck green.

Jenny also had a very loving daddy. Every night when she was ready for bed, her daddy would stop whatever he was doing and come upstairs to read her a story. One night when he finished the story, he said to Jenny, "I love you, sweetheart. Do you love me?"

"Oh yes, Daddy," Jenny replied. "You know that I love you."

"Then give me your pearls," her father said.

Jenny was confused. "Oh, Daddy, not my pearls," she said. "But you can have Princess, the white horse from my collection. Remember, Daddy? The one you gave me last year? She's my favorite."

"That's okay, Honey," Jenny's father said. "Daddy loves you. Good night." And he brushed her cheek with a kiss.

About a week later, after story time, Jenny's daddy said once again, "I sure do love you, sweetheart. Do you love me?"

"Daddy, you know I love you."

"Then give me your pearls."

Jenny was confused again. "Oh Daddy, not my pearls. But you can

have my baby doll. The brand new one I got for my birthday. She is so beautiful. You can have the yellow blanket that matches her sleeper, too."

"That's okay," Jenny's father said. "Daddy loves you. Good night." And as always, he gave her a gentle kiss.

A few nights later when her daddy came in, Jenny was sitting on her bed with her legs crossed. As he came close, he noticed her chin was trembling and one silent tear rolled down her cheek.

"What is it, Jenny? What's the matter?"

Jenny didn't say anything, but lifted her little hand up to her daddy. And when she opened it, there was her little pearl necklace. With a little quiver, she finally said, "Here, Daddy, it's for you."

With tears gathering in his own eyes, Jenny's daddy reached out with one hand to take the necklace. With the other hand he reached into his pocket and pulled out a blue velvet case and gave it to Jenny.

When she opened it, she found a beautiful strand of real pearls.

WHERE TO TAKE IT FROM HERE...

What are you hanging on to? What kind of cheap, dime-store jewelry is preventing you from receiving the blessings that your heavenly Father wants to pour out on you?

Jesus said, "But seek first his kingdom and his righteousness, and all these things will be given to you as well" (Matthew 6:33). If you truly love Jesus and want to follow him, then you must let go of worldly things that seem so important to you and trust that he will give you much more in return.

Maybe it's your friends that are holding you back and keeping you from being the kind of person God wants you to be. The thought of letting them go, of being rejected, of being alone may scare you so much that you refuse to do anything about it. But God is faithful and good. He doesn't want you to be rejected or alone any more than you do. Trust that he will give you back some new friends—better friends—because you've been obedient to him.

Maybe it's wrong or childish thoughts about God. He's not waiting for you to mess up, so he can zap you with zits!

Maybe you're holding onto the fake pearls of popularity or acceptance. You've been desperate to be liked and, until now, have been holding on to fake acceptance from your peers, rather than the unconditional love and unclouded acceptance that God gives.

What's your string of cheap pearls? What feels risky to let go of—even though you know it will be better to go for the perfect pearls?

Through Thick and Thin

The Sydney Swans were the joke of the Australian Rules football league. They had the worst record, the worst players, the worst coach, and the worst fans. Most of their home games were played in front of empty seats.

But a strange thing happened. The team got a new coach and a few new players—and started winning. Before long, the team that had been the laughing stock of the league was a powerhouse.

And since everybody likes a winning team, you can imagine what happened next. The stands began to fill. Thousands of people who had no interest in the team before began to attend games religiously. The Sydney Swans became the talk of the town. Everyone wanted to be identified with them.

Downtown Sydney was awash in the team's colors, and people could be seen wearing Swans merchandise everywhere! Soon it became almost impossible to get a ticket to a Swans game.

One Sunday afternoon the Swans were playing a rival team in front of a capacity crowd. As the TV cameras zoomed in on the revelry and joy in the stands, one focused on a single man who was cheering and waving a sign that he had obviously made himself. Grinning proudly, he held up his sign for all the world to see: I WAS HERE WHEN NOBODY ELSE WAS!

? WHERE TO TAKE IT FROM HERE...

What an awesome picture of Jesus. When you're not winning, when all the odds are stacked against you, when you've become the laughing stock of your school or family, when you feel like the biggest loser of all time, Jesus is cheering you on. He's there when nobody else is. "And surely I am with you always, to the very end of the age" (Matthew 28:20).

A Special Occasion

The following article by Ann Wells appeared several years ago in the *Los Angeles Times:*

My brother-in-law opened the bottom drawer of my sister's bureau and lifted out a tissue-wrapped package. "This," he said, "is not a slip. This is lingerie." He discarded the tissue and handed me the slip. It was exquisite; silk, handmade and trimmed with a cobweb of lace. The price tag with an astronomical figure on it was still attached. "Jan bought this the first time we went to New York, at least 8 or 9 years ago. She never wore it. She was saving it for a special occasion. Well, I guess this is the occasion." He took the slip from me and put it on the bed with the other clothes we were taking to the mortician. His hands lingered on the soft material for a moment, then he slammed the drawer shut and turned to me. "Don't ever save anything for a special occasion. Every day you're alive is a special occasion."

I remembered those words through the funeral and the days that followed when I helped him and my niece attend to all the sad chores that follow an unexpected death. I thought about them on the plane returning to California from the Midwestern town where my sister's family lives. I thought about all the things that she hadn't seen or heard or done. I thought about the things that she had done without realizing that they were special.

I'm still thinking about his words, and they've changed my life. I'm reading more and dusting less. I'm sitting on the deck and admiring the view without fussing about the weeds in the garden. I'm spending more time with my family and friends and less time in committee meetings. Whenever possible, life should be a pattern of experience to savor, not endure. I'm trying to recognize these moments now and cherish them.

I'm not "saving" anything; we use our good china and crystal for every special event—such as losing a pound, getting the sink unstopped, the first camellia blossom.

I wear my good blazer to the market if I feel like it. My theory is if I look prosperous, I can shell out $28.49 for one small bag of groceries without wincing. I'm not saving my good perfume for special parties; clerks in hardware stores and tellers in banks have noses that function as well as my party-going friends.

"Someday" and "one of these days" are losing their grip on my vocabulary. If it's worth seeing or hearing or doing, I want to see and hear and do it now. I'm not sure what my sister would have done had she known that she wouldn't be here for the tomorrow we all take for granted. I think she would have called family members and a few close friends. She might have called a few former friends to apologize and mend fences for past squabbles.

I like to think she would have gone out for a Chinese dinner, her favorite food. I'm guessing—I'll never know.

It's those little things left undone that would make me angry if I knew that my hours were limited. Angry because I put off seeing good friends whom I was going to get in touch with—someday. Angry because I hadn't written certain letters that I intended to write—one of these days. Angry and sorry that I didn't tell my husband and daughter often enough how much I truly love them. I'm trying very hard not to put off, hold back, or save anything that would add laughter and luster to our lives.

And every morning when I open my eyes, I tell myself that the day is special. Every day, every minute, every breath truly is...a gift from God.

 **WHERE TO TAKE IT FROM HERE...**

Life is a precious gift from God, and he wants us to get the most out of it. Jesus came to give us life "to the full" (John 10:10). In other words, he came so that we would live our lives abundantly—full of purpose, meaning, and joy.

Contrary to what some people believe, God wants you to have fun, to live life well—especially while you're young. "Let your heart give you joy in the days of your youth" (Ecclesiastes 11:9). Of course, that doesn't mean you should party all the time or live your life selfishly. Ultimate joy comes from serving God and serving others—from doing what you were created to do.

What are you waiting for? If it's a special occasion or a "someday," keep in mind that it may never come. "Remember your Creator in the days of your youth, before the days of trouble come and the years approach when you will say 'I find no pleasure in them'...Remember him—before the dust returns to the ground it came from, and the spirit returns to God who gave it" (Ecclesiastes 12:1,6-7).

Radical Faith

The following letter was written by a young pastor in Zimbabwe who was later martyred for his faith:

I'm part of the fellowship of the unashamed. I have the Holy Spirit power. The die has been cast. I have stepped over the line. The decision has been made—I'm a disciple of his. I won't look back, let up, slow down, back away, or be still. My past is redeemed, my present makes sense, my future is secure. I'm finished and done with low living, sight walking, smooth knees, colorless dreams, tamed visions, worldly talking, cheap giving, and dwarfed goals.

I no longer need preeminence, prosperity, position, promotions, plaudits, or popularity. I don't have to be right, first, tops, recognized, praised, regarded, or rewarded. I now live by faith, lean on his presence, walk by patience, am uplifted by prayer, and labor with power.

My face is set, my gait is fast, my goal is heaven, my road is narrow, my way is rough, my companions are few, my Guide is reliable, my mission is clear. I cannot be bought, compromised, detoured, lured away, turned back, deluded, or delayed. I will not flinch in the face of sacrifice, hesitate in the presence of the enemy, pander at the pool of popularity, or meander in the maze of mediocrity.

I won't give up, shut up, or let up until I have stayed up, stored up, prayed up, paid up, preached up for the cause of Christ. I am a disciple of Jesus. I must keep going until he comes, give until I drop, preach until all know, and work until he stops me. And, when he comes for his own, he will have no problem recognizing me. My banner will be clear.

 WHERE TO TAKE IT FROM HERE...

Following Christ is not about joining a church or going to youth group activities or listening to Christian music. It's not about wearing Jesus on your T-shirt; it's about being willing to put your life on the line for him. The decision to follow Christ is radical, unequivocal, and unmistakable.

How committed to Jesus are you? Will he recognize you as one of his one when he returns?

What's Your Excuse?

Think you're unqualified to minister to other people? Consider this:

1. Moses stuttered.
2. David's armor didn't fit.
3. John Mark was undependable.
4. Hosea married a prostitute.
5. Amos only had experience as a fig tree pruner.
6. Jacob was a liar.
7. David had an affair.
8. Solomon had too much money.
9. Abraham was too old.
10. Timothy had ulcers.
11. Joseph was a nuisance.
12. Paul was ugly.
13. Peter was a coward.
14. Lazarus was dead.
15. John was self-righteous.
16. Jesus was homeless.
17. Naomi was a widow.
18. Jonah was disobedient.
19. Miriam was a gossip.
20. Gideon and Thomas were doubters.
21. Jeremiah was suicidal.
22. Elijah suffered from depression.
23. Paul was a murderer.
24. So was Moses.
25. Not to mention David.
26. John the Baptist dressed funny.
27. Martha was a worrywart.
28. Samson needed a haircut.
29. Noah had a drinking problem.
30. Moses had a short fuse.
31. Zacchaeus was very short.

32. David was only a teenager.

33. So was Mary, the mother of Jesus.

34. So was Daniel.

35. So were many others who were used by God.

WHERE TO TAKE IT FROM HERE...

Fortunately, God doesn't require a job interview for his ministry. He doesn't do background checks or ask for references. He doesn't care what your qualifications are.

The fact is, no one is qualified to serve God. If you think you're qualified, you'll likely fail. God calls unqualified people because the only way they can be successful in their ministry is to depend completely on him. As God told Moses, "Now go; I will help you speak and will teach you what to say" (Exodus 4:12).

44

Do Something!

St. Michael's had always been a very wealthy church. Its 300 members usually gave a combined annual offering of over one million dollars—because they could afford to.

Over the years, however, the neighborhood around the beautiful old church began to change. Immigrants flocked to the area, changing the

complexion of the community. Steel bars replaced welcome signs in store windows. Homeless people could be found wandering the sidewalks and streets. The changes made some members of St. Michael's very uncomfortable. They usually tried to avoid that part of town except on Sundays.

One Sunday, shortly after a young associate priest had joined the church staff, the church members were gathered after the morning service for coffee and pastries. In the spring months they loved to gather in the flower garden outside the church, among its gazebos, fountains, and vine-covered arches.

As the elegantly dressed worshipers sipped coffee and chatted in the garden, a homeless man shuffled in off the street. He entered through the garden gate without looking at anyone. But all eyes were certainly on him. He quietly walked over to the table where a spread of expensive pastries were displayed on silver trays. He picked up one of the pastries and bit into it, keeping his eyes closed.

Then he reached for a second pastry and placed it into his coat pocket. Moving slowly and trying not to be noticed, he placed another into the same pocket.

The garden buzzed with whispers. Finally one of the women walked over to the new priest and said, "Well, do something!"

Still feeling a little awkward in his new position, the young priest handed his coffee cup to the woman, walked over to the table, and stood next to the homeless man. He reached under the table, where the empty pastry boxes had been stored. Then he picked up one of the silver trays loaded with pastries and emptied them into a box. He did the same with a second tray of expensive goodies. Then he closed the lids on the boxes and held them out to the homeless man.

"We're here every Sunday," the priest said.

The man smiled at the priest, cradled the boxes in his arms, and shuffled quietly out of the garden and down the street.

The priest returned to his coffee cup, smiled at the woman holding it, and said, "That's what you meant when you said, 'Do something,' wasn't it?"

 WHERE TO TAKE IT FROM HERE...

What would you have done if you'd been that priest?

That's an important question for all of us. Jesus looks out at the homeless and weak of this world and says to each of us, "Well, do something."

Certainly if Jesus were here in the flesh, you can bet he would have done something very much like what that young priest did.

But wait! Jesus is here in the flesh. That's what the church is all about. We are the body of Christ—the hands and feet of Jesus in today's world (1 Corinthians 12).

46

Bobby's Valentines

Bobby was a special-education boy. He was just bright enough to remain in a regular classroom but was still noticeably different. He was the constant butt of jokes by his classmates, but he never seemed to mind. Every day, as the neighborhood kids walked home from school, Bobby's mother would look out the window to see them all laughing and joking together—all except Bobby. He was always walking behind the others, all alone. It was obvious that the other children felt uncomfortable around Bobby and shunned him.

One day Bobby burst into the kitchen after school. "Mom, guess what?" he said. "Valentine's Day is two weeks away, and our teacher said we could make valentines and give them to the other kids in our class!"

His mother's heart sank as she pictured yet another opportunity for Bobby to be excluded. "Mom," Bobby continued, "I'm going to make a valentine for every person in my class!"

"That's very nice, Bobby," his mother answered, fighting back the tears.

Over the next two weeks, Bobby worked every afternoon on those valentines. They were truly labors of love. When the big day finally came, he was so excited about taking his valentines to school that he couldn't eat breakfast. But he was also a little worried.

"I hope I didn't forget anybody," he said as he dashed off to school.

Bobby's mother made a fresh batch of his favorite cookies and prepared herself to comfort her son when he returned home brokenhearted from the valentine exchange. She knew how disappointed he would be with the response he got from the other children.

That afternoon she saw the same cluster of neighborhood kids walking home together. A half block behind them, all alone, was Bobby. Bobby's mother turned away and placed a plate of cookies on the table.

Much to her surprise, Bobby came through the door with a huge smile on his face. "What is it, Bobby?" she asked. "How did it go?"

With a shout of pure joy, Bobby said, "Guess what, Mom! I didn't forget a single kid!"

 WHERE TO TAKE IT FROM HERE...

Bobby was so focused on giving that he didn't consider the response he would get. He was so concerned about others that he was blind to the fact that he was being slighted.

Sometimes when we give, our motive is to make people think we're wonderful or to prompt others to give something in return. But that's not the way of Christ.

Jesus gave his life for us knowing that we would "not receive him" (John 1:11). That's agape, God's love. It is unconditional, unselfish, and given with no strings attached. "For God so loved the world that he gave..." (John 3:16), and he didn't forget a single one of us.

May we all be more like Bobby.

Clever Hans

In the early 1900s, a German named Herr von Osten trained his horse Hans to count by tapping his front hoof. Apparently Hans was a quick learner, because von Osten soon had him performing amazing feats in front of paying audiences.

Hans demonstrated a talent for adding, subtracting, dividing, and performing complex mathematical calculations. He was even able to count the number of people in a room or the number of people wearing eyeglasses.

As his fame grew, he became known as Clever Hans, the smartest horse in the world. But there were doubters. Some accused von Osten of deceiving the public by using trickery and sleight of hand to make money. They demanded proof of Hans' mathematical abilities.

The first test the doubters came up with involved calculating numbers that were randomly selected on stage by people other than von Osten. Using his hoof, Hans pounded out the correct answers every time. Some of the doubters started to believe that the horse was indeed a mathematical genius.

Then came the second test. In this one, one person whispered a number in Hans's left ear and another person whispered a number in his right ear. Hans was told to add the two numbers and pound out the sum. He couldn't do it.

On further investigation, it was found that Hans could solve problems only if someone he could see knew the answer.

When Hans was given numbers and asked to compute them, spectators leaned forward and tensed their bodies as Hans began tapping his hoof. When Hans had tapped the correct number, onlookers relaxed their body postures and nodded their heads, which was Hans's signal to stop tapping. Hans was indeed clever—not because he could calculate, but because he could read human body language!

? WHERE TO TAKE IT FROM HERE...

Clever Hans could figure out the correct answers to complex mathematical equations simply by watching people. If someone were watching you that closely, what would they discover? Specifically, what would they discover about following Christ?

You don't have to say a word about following Christ to let people know what kind of difference he's made in your life. All you have to do is live. As St. Francis of Assisi once said: "Preach the Gospel at all times. If necessary, use words."

Our actions, body language, and nonverbal communication often do the talking for us. And when our actions contradict our words, our actions win out every time.

The question has been asked, "If you were arrested for being a follower of Jesus, would there be enough evidence to convict you?" Sadly, many Christians betray Jesus not with their words but with their disobedience.

Jason's Worst Christmas

More than anything else Jason wanted a new PlayStation system for Christmas. Forget about clothes or CDs or money. His only hope for finding holiday fulfillment was a PlayStation.

Jason's mom and dad both worked, so he always got home from school two hours before they got home. One afternoon while he was home by himself, he wandered into his parents' bedroom, wondering what he might find.

He looked in the closet, opened a few drawers, and then peeked under the bed. He found a shopping bag from an electronics store—the same one that sold PlayStation systems!

He knew he shouldn't look. His parents had hidden the shopping bag under their bed for a reason. They wanted to surprise him on Christmas morning.

Jason decided not to look. He left his parents' bedroom and went to his own room. But his mind kept returning to that shopping bag under the bed. It had his PlayStation system in it, he was sure of that. It's going to be mine in a few weeks anyway, he reasoned, so why shouldn't I have it now? He tortured himself with thoughts like that for the rest of the night.

By the time he got home from school the next afternoon, Jason couldn't stand it any longer. He headed straight for his parents' bed and looked inside the bag. His suspicion was confirmed: it was a brand new PlayStation.

Jason carefully removed the box from the bag and held it on his lap for a while. He didn't try to open it at first because he was afraid he wouldn't be able to get it closed again. He just stared at the picture on the front and read all of the fine print. He also tried to talk himself out of what he knew he was going to do.

But the temptation proved too much for him.

Jason carefully broke the seals on the box and slid the console out. With just a moment's hesitation, he hooked it up to the TV and played

with it for about ten minutes.

He had fun, but not as much fun as he'd imagined. Maybe he was too scared of being caught to enjoy himself. He put everything back in the box exactly as he had found it and replaced the box in the shopping bag under the bed.

Jason did the same thing the next day—and every day for the next three weeks. He would come home, take the PlayStation out, and play with it a little longer each day. But he always managed to put it away just before his parents got home from work.

When Christmas finally came, Jason's parents put his present under the tree, but Jason found it hard to get excited. He already knew what he was getting, and while it was just what he'd asked for, it didn't feel right. When the time came to open his gift, he tried to act surprised (for his parents' sake), but it was no big deal to him. In fact, it was a huge disappointment.

It was Jason's worst Christmas ever.

 WHERE TO TAKE IT FROM HERE...

Jason's parents would have been very upset if they had known what he was doing. Perhaps that's how God feels when he sees us open his gift of sex before marriage. Obviously he wants us to have the gift, but he wants us to wait until the proper time.

God created sex for marriage, to be enjoyed by a husband and wife who love each other for a lifetime. God isn't trying to make life miserable for you. He wants you to enjoy it (and sex) to the fullest—according to his plan.

It's understandable that Jason was disappointed with his PlayStation game after he opened it. The anticipation was gone; and he felt guilt, shame, and worry. He would have enjoyed the game a whole lot more if he had just been patient

The same goes for sex. Why settle for temporary, muted pleasure when you can experience the pleasure God intended just by waiting? Why spoil everything for yourself and your future spouse?

The Cracked Pot

Many years ago a rich man had a servant whose job was to carry water each day from a distant stream to his master's house.

The servant carried the water in two large pots, each of which hung from opposite ends of a pole he carried across his neck. One pot was in perfect condition and always delivered a full portion of water at the end of the long walk from the stream. The other pot had a crack in it, though, and always arrived at the master's house half full.

For two years the servant delivered only one and a half pots of water to his master's house each day. The undamaged pot was proud of itself. It had been made to carry water without leaking, and it did the job perfectly. The cracked pot, on the other hand, felt ashamed. It was miserable knowing it was not able to accomplish what it had been made to do. Still, it did the best it could, even if it was only half of what the perfect pot could do.

Finally the cracked pot spoke to the servant one day by the stream. "I need to apologize to you," the pot said, "For two years now, I have been able to deliver only half my load because this crack in my side causes water to leak out all the way back to your master's house. Because of my flaws you have to do all of this work, and you don't get full value for your efforts."

The servant simply said, "When we return to the master's house, I want you to notice the beautiful flowers along the path."

As they made their way back to the house, the cracked pot saw the gorgeous wildflowers beside the path and was cheered a little by their beauty.

When they reached the house, the servant said to the cracked pot, "Did you notice that there were flowers only on your side of the path?

I've always known about your flaw, and I took advantage of it. I planted flower seeds on your side of the path. Every day when we walked back from the stream, you watered them. For two years I've been able to pick these beautiful flowers to decorate my master's table. If you weren't just the way you are, he would not have this beauty to grace his house."

? WHERE TO TAKE IT FROM HERE...

Each of us has our own unique flaws. You might say we're all a bunch of crackpots. But if we will allow him to, the Lord will use our flaws to grace his table.

In God's great economy, nothing goes to waste. The Lord knows what your shortcomings are, and he will use them to his own advantage—and to your advantage, as well. He'll throw some flower seeds in your path and give you a chance to water them along the way.

Don't be ashamed or afraid of your flaws. Instead, celebrate them and remember that God has always used imperfect people to accomplish his perfect will. Paul wrote, "If I must boast, I will boast of the things that show my weakness" (2 Corinthians 11:30). Paul had quite a few flaws, which he freely acknowledged, but God still used him in a mighty way. He can use you as well.

The CPR Class

When Gordon accepted the youth pastor position at his church, he learned that the job required CPR training. Reluctantly he signed up for a class offered by the local YMCA.

Gordon felt a little uncomfortable in the class at first but decided to make the best of it. When things got a little boring, he entertained the class—and irritated the instructor—with a few jokes.

Even though he didn't take the instruction seriously, he managed to pass the CPR exam. He became a certified lifesaver, though he had very little confidence in his ability to actually save someone's life.

A few weeks later Gordon was driving to work when he witnessed a traffic accident. He jumped out of his car to see if he could help. Someone yelled, "Does anybody here know CPR?"

Nervously, Gordon answered, "I do!" and stepped to the front. There was a man on the ground who appeared to be unconscious. Gordon told someone to call 911 and quickly examined the victim. He checked to see if the man was breathing and found nothing.

Gordon knew that he was supposed to administer quick breaths and force air into the man's lungs. But at that moment the reality of the situation hit him.

What am I doing here? he wondered. I can't do this! I don't remember a thing from that silly CPR class!

Gordon backed away for several seconds to collect his thoughts. That's when he noticed just how dirty and disgusting the man was.

There's no way I can give him mouth-to-mouth resuscitation, Gordon decided.

Then the gravity of the situation overtook him. The man was dying, and Gordon had to do something. Gordon knelt down, cupped his mouth over the man's, and began giving him quick breaths. He checked for a pulse and found that the man's heart was beating. He checked for breathing. Still nothing. The man wasn't getting oxygen. Gordon gave him more quick, forceful breaths. Dozens of onlookers encouraged him. Some of them prayed.

After what seemed like an eternity, the man on the ground finally started breathing on his own. About that time, a team of paramedics arrived on the scene. The paramedics thanked Gordon and assured him that the man was going to live.

Gordon walked away from the incident feeling overwhelmed. Despite the fact that he'd felt completely inadequate and unprepared to save someone's life, he had actually done it. He thought of his CPR class and how he'd considered it a waste of time.

As it turned out, Gordon was wrong about that.

 WHERE TO TAKE IT FROM HERE...

Do you ever get the feeling that going to church, reading your Bible, and praying are complete wastes of time? Do those activities seem boring and irrelevant to you? Do you ever wonder how you can apply a sermon principle or a Bible verse to your life?

Gordon found himself prepared to save a man's life in spite of himself. That same type of surprise may await you. Someday you will face an unexpected, stressful, and seemingly impossible situation. You may feel overwhelmed by the real challenges of life. But you'll be prepared in spite of yourself. The time you spend now learning and growing in the faith will pay off big time later. You can count on it. (2 Timothy 2:15; 4:2; Ephesians 2:10)

A Great Man

History records that he was great man. Yet he had humble beginnings. He grew up in a small village, an ordinary boy who did nothing to draw attention to himself.

Like most boys his age, he attended school. He also worked in the family business and did his best to grow up strong and healthy. Deep inside, however, he knew he had a special purpose, a destiny to fulfill.

As he grew older people began to notice that there was something special about this young man. He had talent and charisma. He was gifted like no other. It wasn't long before he started attracting crowds. Thousands came to see and listen to him.

He chose a small band of loyal companions who traveled with him everywhere he went. Many of them had given up their jobs just to be with their idol and take care of his needs.

As his fame spread, some grew jealous of him. Others thought he was leading people astray, and they plotted against him. But his popularity only increased. He touched the lives of young and old alike and brought joy and laughter to the weak and downhearted. Many hailed him as king.

Toward the end of his short life, he suffered quite a bit. Some who had followed him fell away and turned to worshiping others.

He died alone. Those closest to him were left discouraged and confused. They never expected his life to end that way.

Soon after his death, there were rumors that he didn't really die. His followers spread the news all around. "He lives!" they said. "He is not dead!" Some claimed they actually saw him. Even today, many believe he is still alive.

By now, you've probably figured out who this great man was.

His name was Elvis Presley.

(?) WHERE TO TAKE IT FROM HERE...

If you word things generally enough, you can find a lot of similarities between Jesus and Elvis. In fact, you can find a lot of similarities between Jesus and you. That's because Jesus was a human being, just like you. He was fully God, but he was also fully human.

That's where the similarities end, however. Elvis came to sing; Jesus came to save.

There is only one Jesus Christ, Son of God, who was born of a virgin, died on a cross for the sins of the world, rose again on the third day, and today sits at the right hand of the Father, making intercession for everyone who calls on his name.

While others have been hailed as "king," there is only one "King of King and Lord of Lords." His name is Jesus.

Fighting Fire with Fire

The pioneers who settled the American West often had to travel for days at a time across miles and miles of grassy plains. And while pioneers considered mountain ranges difficult and treacherous to cross, they dreaded these vast plains even more. It wasn't hostile Indians, prairie wolves, rattlesnakes, or summer heat that caused their fear. It was lightning.

The high grass on the plains was often so dry that lightning could ignite a small fire that could then be whipped up by the winds and spread quickly across the land, engulfing everything and everyone in its path. Many died on their journeys across the plains simply because they were unable to outrun a raging prairie fire.

After many tragic journeys, the pioneers developed a method of finding refuge from these fires that is still used today. Whenever they saw smoke from a lightning fire in the distance, they would go downwind from their wagons and set the plains on fire. The wind would then push that fire and burn the grass downwind from them. Once the grass was burned, they would then move their horses and wagons across the scorched land. When the fire from the lightning did reach them, they were safe because there was no longer any grass to be burned.

The pioneers found safety by fighting fire with fire.

 WHERE TO TAKE IT FROM HERE...

In a sense, Jesus fought fire with fire. He took the sins of the world upon himself and endured a cruel death so that we would not have to suffer the fires of hell. Jesus knew the only way for us to avoid death was for him to die. By taking our sins to the cross, he destroyed them "as far as the east is from the west" (Psalm 103:12) and provided us with a safe place to stand. "Therefore, there is now no condemnation for those who are in Christ Jesus" (Romans 8:1).

Don't try to outrun the flames. You can't do it. You need to stand firm on the solid rock of faith in Jesus Christ.

THE LIST

In his book *Serving God*, Ben Patterson tells this story:

Once upon a time a woman was married to a perfectionist husband. No matter what his wife did for him, it was never enough. At the beginning of each day, he would make out his list of chores for her to do, and at the end of each day, he would scrutinize it to make sure she had done all that she was supposed to do. The best compliment she ever received was a disinterested grunt if she finished everything. She grew to hate her husband. When he died unexpectedly, she was embarrassed to admit to herself that she was relieved.

Within a year of her husband's death, she met a warm and loving man who was everything her former husband was not. They fell deeply in love with each other and were married. Every day they spent together seemed better than the day before.

One afternoon, as she was cleaning out boxes in the attic, a crumpled piece of paper caught her eye. It was one of the old chore lists that her first husband used to make out for her. In spite of her chagrin, she couldn't help reading it again. To her shock and amazement she discovered that, without even thinking about it, she was now doing for her new husband all the things she used to hate to do for her old husband. Her new husband never once suggested that she do any of these things. But she was doing them anyway—because she loved him.

Do you ever think of the Christian life as nothing more than a list of "thou shalts" and "thou shalt nots"?

That's not what Jesus intended. In fact, he came to put an end to the long list of laws and regulations that governed Israel for so many years. He came with a new law, the law of love. He said, "Love the Lord your God with all your heart and with your soul and with all your mind" (Matthew 22:37).

If you love God, you'll do the right things—not because you're afraid of breaking the law, but because you want to do them.

The Christian faith has little to do with laws and lists. But it has everything to do with love. When Peter needed forgiveness and healing after he denied Christ, Jesus asked him only one question: "Do you truly love me?" (John 21:15). We must answer the same question, too.

Do you love Jesus? If you do, you'll gladly serve him and obey his commands.

Timmy's Flower

"Today we are going to draw a picture," Timmy's kindergarten teacher announced.

Good, Timmy thought. He liked to draw pictures. He could draw lions and tigers and trains and boats. He took out his crayons and began to draw.

But the teacher said, "Wait, it's not time to begin." She paused until everyone looked ready. "Now," she said, "we are going to draw flowers."

Good, Timmy thought. He began to draw beautiful flowers with his orange and pink and blue crayons.

But the teacher said, "Wait." She drew a picture of a flower on the blackboard. It was red with a green stem. "There," she said, "now you may begin."

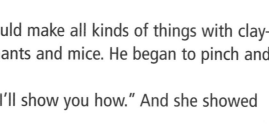

Timmy looked at his teacher's flower. He liked his better, but he didn't say anything. He just turned his paper over and made a flower like the teacher's. It was red with a green stem.

A few days later the teacher said, "Today we are going to make something with clay."

Good, Timmy thought. He could make all kinds of things with clay—snakes and snowmen and elephants and mice. He began to pinch and pull his ball of clay.

But the teacher said, "Wait, I'll show you how." And she showed everyone how to make a dish.

So Timmy rolled his clay into a ball, flattened it, and made a dish like the teacher's.

Timmy learned to wait and watch and make things just like the teacher's. And pretty soon he stopped making creations of his own.

Then one day Timmy's family moved to another city, and Timmy started at a new school. On his first day, Timmy's new teacher said, "Today we are going to draw a picture."

Good, Timmy thought. And he waited for the teacher to tell him what to do. But the teacher didn't say anything. She just walked around the room. When she came to Timmy, she said, "Don't you want to draw a picture?"

"Yes," said Timmy. "What are we going to draw?"

"Well, I don't know until you draw it," the teacher said.

"How should I make it?" he asked.

"Why, any way you like."

"And any color?"

"Any color," the teacher said. "If everyone drew the same thing in the same color, how would I know who made what?"

"I don't know," said Timmy. And he began to draw a flower.

It was red with a green stem.

? ████ WHERE TO TAKE IT FROM HERE... ████

When Timmy was very young, he was robbed of his creativity. His teacher told him that there was only one way to draw a flower or shape a lump of clay.

You may be more like Timmy than you realize. You have the potential to draw outside the lines, to be creative, to use your talents and gifts in a remarkable and unique way, but the world has told you that you can't do it.

The world we live in conditions us at an early age to believe that we all have to look the same, act the same, and think the same. Then when Jesus calls us to be different, we find it difficult, if not impossible, to respond to his call.

"Do not conform any longer to the pattern of this world, but be transformed by the renewing of your mind" (Romans 12:2). If you will allow Jesus to have control of your life, you can break out of the world's mold and become what God created you to be.

On The Right Track

Wilbert Awdry was the son of a poor preacher in Wiltshire, England. As a boy he often accompanied his father on his visiting rounds. Wilbert especially liked riding the train and talking to the railway workers he met along the way.

A poor student, Wilbert barely managed to finish college. He decided to follow in his father's footsteps because he liked the idea of helping people see God. But Wilbert was not a successful pastor. In fact he was fired by his church and for a while considered leaving the ministry altogether.

But then an event took place that changed his life forever. Wilbert's first child, Christopher, caught the measles. While Christopher was confined to his bed, Pastor Awdry amused him with a story he'd made up about a little train engine who was sad because he hadn't been out of his shed for a long time.

The boy wanted to hear the story over and over again. Wilbert finally wrote it down and illustrated it with some crude line drawings of trains with faces on them.

Wilbert's wife saw more in the little story than family entertainment. She pushed her husband to offer the book to a publisher. Much to Wilbert's surprise, the publisher liked it.

In 1945, Wilbert Awdry's first book, *The Three Railway Engines*, was published.

Book after book followed. All were stories about little train engines with different personalities who interacted in very simple, but very human, dramas. Every story rang with a message of morality, grace, and redemption.

As Awdry himself said of his creation, "The important thing is that the engines are punished and forgiven—but never scrapped!"

Wilbert Awdry wasn't very successful as a church pastor. But he has been extremely successful in sharing the love of God in another setting. Ask any child if they've heard of Pastor Awdry's creation, *Thomas the Tank Engine*, and you'll see just how successful he's been.

When he was asked what he would like to have engraved on his tombstone, he replied, "He helped people see God in the ordinary things of life...and he made children laugh." Not a bad legacy. Wilbert Awdry went to be with the Lord in March of 1997.

? **WHERE TO TAKE IT FROM HERE...**

What will your legacy be? Each of us is called by God to serve and glorify him in all we do. That doesn't mean you have to become a pastor or a missionary or go into full-time Christian service. You can serve God doing whatever you do best.

If you're an artist, you can create art to the glory of God. If you're a construction worker, you can build buildings to the glory of God. If you're a burger flipper, you can flip burgers to the glory of God. And if you do, you can be certain that you'll leave a legacy.

"And whatever you do, whether in word or deed, do it all in the name of the Lord Jesus, giving thanks to God the Father through him" (Colossians 3:17).

Just Some Old Birds

Murmurs rippled through the congregation when Reverend George Thomas placed a rusty old bird cage on the pulpit. The church members weren't used to their pastor using props in his sermons—especially not on Easter Sunday.

Sensing the congregation's confusion, Reverend Thomas explained how he had obtained the cage.

It seems that the day before he had been walking through town when he noticed a young boy carelessly swinging the cage around. Thomas noticed that there were three obviously frightened little birds inside the cage.

The pastor stopped the youngster and asked, "What have you got there, son?"

"Just some old birds," came the reply.

"And what are you going to do with them," he asked.

"Take 'em home and have some fun with 'em," the boy said. "I'm gonna poke 'em and pull out their feathers and watch 'em fight. I'm gonna have a real good time."

"But those birds don't belong to you," said the pastor.

"They do now," the boy responded. "I found 'em and I can do anything I want with 'em."

"But you'll get tired of playing with those birds, son. What will you do with them then?"

"Oh, I've got some cats," grinned the boy. "They like birds. I'll give 'em to my cats."

The pastor was silent for a moment. Then he asked, "How much do you want for those birds, son?"

"You don't want these birds, mister," said the boy. "They're just plain old field birds. They don't sing. They ain't even pretty."

"How much?"

The boy sized up the pastor as if he were crazy and said, "Ten bucks."

The pastor reached into his pocket and took out a ten dollar bill. He placed it in the boy's hand. In a flash, the boy was gone. The pastor set the cage down, opened the door, and gently coaxed the birds out, setting them free.

The congregation listened quietly as the pastor told of his encounter with the boy. Then he told them another story.

One day Jesus and the devil were having a conversation. Satan had just come from the Garden of Eden, grinning and boasting. "I just caught me a bunch of people down there. Set me a trap! Used bait I knew they couldn't resist! Got 'em all!"

"What are you going to do with them?" Jesus asked.

"Oh, I'm gonna have fun with them. I'm gonna teach them how to hurt and abuse each other. I'll teach them how to marry and divorce each other, lie to each other, and kill each other. Oh, I'm gonna really have a good time!"

"But those people don't belong to you," said Jesus.

"They do now! I can do anything I want with them."

"And what will you do when you get through with them?" asked Jesus.

"I'll kill them."

"How much do you want for them?"

"Oh, you don't want these people," said the devil. "They're no good. You may love them, sure, but they'll just hate you back. They'll spit on you, curse you, and kill you. You don't want these people."

"How much?" Jesus asked.

Satan sized up Jesus as if he were crazy and said, "Your life."

The pastor ended his story this way: "Jesus paid the price. And on that first Easter Sunday morning, he picked up the cage, opened the door, and set us free."

(?) WHERE TO TAKE IT FROM HERE...

"It is for freedom that Christ has set us free. Stand firm, then, and do not let yourselves be burdened again by a yoke of slavery" (Galatians 5:1).

DO YOU KNOW ME?

A history professor at a large university was giving a final exam to his freshman class. When the two-hour time limit was up, he announced that the test was over and that students should place their booklets in a pile on his desk.

The professor sat back in his chair and watched as the 250 students in the auditorium filed past his desk, dropped their tests off, and exited the room. Some grumbled about the difficulty of the exam; others walked out in stunned silence.

As he prepared to sort through the three large piles of tests on his desk, the professor noticed that one young man was still in his seat, working away.

The professor cleared his throat loudly, but the student didn't seem to notice.

The teacher called to the student, "Young man, the test is over! Come down here now and hand in your booklet!"

The student didn't even look up.

The professor decided to teach the young man a lesson. He sat back down at his desk and waited. When the student came up to turn in his examination, the professor planned to rip it to shreds and give him an "F" for the semester.

Five minutes went by. Then ten. Finally, after twenty minutes, the student closed his test booklet and made his way down to the now-fuming professor.

"I'm finished," he said.

"Do you think I'm going to accept your exam now?" the professor asked incredulously.

The young man leaned forward, looking over the stacks of tests on the desk. His eyes narrowed and he frowned just slightly.

"Do you have any idea who you're talking to?" the boy asked.

"I don't know, and I don't care!" the professor spat back.

"Good," said the student. And with that, he stuck his test right in the middle of one of the stacks and walked out.

There are times when it pays to be anonymous. You can get away with all kinds of things if nobody knows who you are.

Many people think they can get away with sin. They assume that with so many people in the world, God couldn't possibly care about one individual. He's too busy running the universe. He's got more important things to do. Besides, who could keep track of billions of people every minute of the day?

That would be God. It's hard for us to relate to that kind of power, because we can't be in more than one place at one time. We can't keep more than one thought in our heads at one time. Some of us can barely walk and chew gum at the same time.

We figure that if God is busy helping a missionary in Africa right now, he certainly can't be paying much attention to us. But he can.

God is omnipresent, omnipotent, and omniscient. He completely fills up the world with his presence, knowledge, and power. He can be completely involved in your life, giving you his undivided attention—and do the same for someone else at the same time thousands of miles away.

We aren't required to understand how he does it. All we're required to do is have faith. Believe and trust that God knows your name, your heart, and all about you—not because he's a cosmic snoop who wants to invade your privacy or a cosmic cop who wants to toss you into hell.

God knows you because he loves you. He wants the best for you. He wants to have a relationship with you. (See Psalm 139.)

The Carpenter's Gift

Grandpa Nybakken loved life, especially when he could play a trick on somebody. At those times his large Norwegian frame would shake with laughter while he feigned innocent surprise, exclaiming, "Oh, forever-more!" But on a cold Saturday in downtown Chicago, God played a trick on him.

Grandpa Nybakken worked as a carpenter. On this particular day, he volunteered to build some crates to hold the clothes his church was sending to an orphanage in China. When he finished building the crates, he helped pack them full of clothing and load them on the trucks that would take them to the shipping docks. He felt good that he could contribute to the project, even in a small way.

On his way home, he reached into his shirt pocket to find his glasses. They were gone. He mentally replayed his earlier actions and realized what had happened. The glasses had slipped out of his pocket unnoticed and fallen into one of the crates. His brand new glasses were heading for China!

The old carpenter had very little money, certainly not enough to replace his glasses. He was upset at the thought of having to buy another pair. "It's not fair," he told God as he drove home in frustration. "I've been very faithful in giving of my time to your work, and now this happens."

Several months later, the director of the Chinese orphanage came to speak at the old carpenter's small church. He began by thanking the people for their faithfulness in supporting the orphanage.

"But most of all," he said, "I must thank you for the glasses you sent last year. You see, the Communists had just swept through the orphanage, destroying everything, including my glasses. I was desperate. Even if I had the money, there was simply no way to replace those glasses. My coworkers and I were much in prayer about the situation. Then your crates arrived. When my staff removed one of the covers, they found a pair of glasses lying on top."

The missionary paused long enough to let his words sink in. Then, still gripped with the wonder of it all, he continued, "Folks, when I tried on the glasses, it was as though they had been custom-made for me! I want to thank you for your thoughtfulness and generosity!"

The congregation listened, pleased about the miraculous glasses. But the missionary surely must have confused their church with another, they thought. There were no eyeglasses on their list of items to be sent overseas.

But sitting quietly in the back, with tears streaming down his face, was an ordinary carpenter who on an ordinary day was used in an extraordinary way by the Master Carpenter himself.

? WHERE TO TAKE IT FROM HERE...

God can use us in ways we might not expect. Even when things go wrong, we can trust that "in all things God works for the good of those who love him, who have been called according to his purpose" (Romans 8:28).

It's hard to explain why bad things happen to God's people. But we can expect that they will. Rain falls on good people the same way it falls on bad people (Matthew 5:45). As Christians, what sustains us is knowing that God is capable of turning the bad into good. He just asks us to trust him.

The Carpenter's Gift was first published as "The Perfect Mistake" in *Chicken Soup for the Christian Family Soul*, copyright © 2000 by Health Communications. Story reprinted by permission of Cheryl Walterman Stewart.

True Confessions

Three longtime friends were out fishing on a boat. After a couple hours without so much as a nibble, they were starting to get bored.

"I've got an idea," the first man said. "Let's be totally honest with each other and confess our worst sins. I'll go first. I have a big problem with the sin of lust. I've been cheating on my wife for over a year. I just can't seem to control myself."

The second man said, "As long as we're being honest with each other, I'll tell you what my problem is. It's the sin of greed. I just can't get enough money, so I've been embezzling funds from my company for years. I just can't seem to control myself."

The third man said, "Well, my problem is the sin of gossip. Not only can't I control myself, I can't wait to get home!"

 WHERE TO TAKE IT FROM HERE...

Confession may be good for the soul, but God is the only one who can forgive us. He does more than just listen; he also forgives, heals, restores, and saves you from the consequences of your sin. What's more, he can provide you with the power you need to overcome temptation and live a holy life.

Go to God with your sins and believe in his Son, who died to set you free from sin's power. "If we confess our sins, he is faithful and just to forgive us our sins and purify us from all unrighteousness" (1 John 1:9).

Early Flubber

During World War II an engineer at General Electric named James Wright was searching for a synthetic rubber substitute. In one of his experiments, he poured boric acid into a test tube filled with silicone oil, and it became a soft, malleable substance.

Imagine his surprise when he dropped a glob of the substance on the floor—and it bounced! With a little more investigation, Wright discovered that the substance could also be stretched, flattened, rolled, and sculpted into many different shapes.

Around the General Electric labs, the substance became something of a novelty. Soon many GE employees were taking some home to show their family and friends.

Unfortunately, the new substance proved to have a rather short shelf life, which made it useless for engineering purposes. It was dismissed by the GE engineers as an interesting, but worthless, discovery.

But a writer named Peter Hodgson became intrigued with the amazing substance after he saw it demonstrated at a party.

Hodgson, a copywriter for a toy catalog, had a feeling that the failed rubber substitute would be extremely popular with children, even if it was not useful for engineers.

After testing the material for safety, Hodgson packaged the stuff in plastic eggs and added a name to it. Within months the weird rubber known as *Silly Putty* became one of the hottest-selling toys in American history.

What looks completely worthless to one person may be extremely valuable to another. It's all a matter of perspective.

For example, others may put you down because you seem worthless to them; however, God has a purpose and plan for your life that no one may be able to see right now.

When Jesus came as Savior of the world, he was rejected by his own people. Even today, people reject him. But as the apostle Paul pointed out, "The message of the cross is foolishness to those who are perishing, but to us who are being saved it is the power of God" (1 Corinthians 1:18).

What looks foolish to the world is wisdom to those who can see things from God's perspective.

74

Old Habits

The French Revolution was tough on nobility. For years the people with money and power in France ignored and humiliated the common people, forcing them to suffer and starve while the noblemen lived in luxury.

With the revolution came payback.

The guillotine was the method of choice for the people's revenge. During the revolution, many noblemen tried to escape execution by disguising themselves to slip out of the country undetected.

One of them, the Marquis de Condonset, donned the ragged clothes of a peasant and attempted to work his way to the nearest border. His ploy worked until he stopped at an inn full of real peasants.

The disguised nobleman walked into the inn, sat down at a table, and ordered an omelet made with a dozen eggs.

That wasn't a smart thing to do in front of a group of people who never would have been able to afford such an extravagant meal.

The nobleman's mistake ended up sending him to the guillotine.

WHERE TO TAKE IT FROM HERE...

It's not easy to pretend to be something you're not. Sooner or later, the real you will come to the surface and expose you for what you really are.

This is especially true of people who pretend to be Christians. Sooner or later, the truth will come out.

Becoming a Christian involves being born again—being changed from the inside out. Only when Christ changes your heart can you truly begin to act like a Christian. You can't wear a Christian disguise. When you've been reborn, your life will begin to show it. Your actions become the evidence of the change that's taken place in your heart (James 2:18). Faith without actions is just as phony as actions without faith.

too BUSY

A seminary professor had a class of fifteen students who were preparing for Christian ministry. At the beginning of one of his classes, he distributed envelopes to the students with sealed instructions.

Five students received instructions to proceed across the campus without delay. The directions read, "You have 15 minutes to reach your destination. You have no time to spare. Don't loiter or do anything else, or your grade will be docked."

The next five students also received instructions to make their way across the campus, but they were given 45 minutes to do so. "You have plenty of time," their directions read, "but don't be too slow."

The last five students received instructions to get to the other side of campus anytime before five o'clock, giving them about five hours to complete the assignment.

What the students didn't know was that the professor had arranged for several drama majors from a nearby university to position themselves along the path that led across campus. The drama students were instructed to act as though they were suffering and in great need.

One pretended to be homeless, in need of food and clothing. Another sat with his head in his hands, crying as if he had just experienced a terrible tragedy. Still another acted as if he were in desperate need of medical care.

You can imagine what happened as the Christian ministry students tried to complete their assignments. None of the students in the first group stopped to offer any help to the "needy people." Only two students in the second group did. But all five students in the third group took time to stop and help.

 WHERE TO TAKE IT FROM HERE...

In today's hectic world, it's no wonder that many people find it hard to do what God wants. Most of them are just too busy. But is that busyness simply an unavoidable part of modern living—or is it sin?

Each of has a choice as to how we will live our lives. We can choose to make room for God and the ministry he has called us to—or we can choose other things...and face the consequences later.

The Inheritance

Two old friends bumped into one another on the street one day. One man looked very sad and discouraged, almost on the verge of tears. His friend asked, "What has the world done to you, my old friend?"

The sad fellow said, "Three weeks ago, a rich uncle of mine died. To my surprise, he included me in his will. His lawyers sent me a check for $40,000!"

"That's terrific," said the friend. "That's a lot of money."

"Yes, but two weeks ago, they sent me another check—this time for $100,000!"

"Wow, that's incredible!" said the friend. "You've really been blessed!"

"You don't understand," the man whined. "Last week I got another check in the mail that was larger than the first two. It was for a quarter of a million dollars!"

The friend was getting very confused. "You're right, I don't understand. Why then are you so unhappy? Why do you look so glum?"

"Because this week I haven't received anything," came the reply.

? WHERE TO TAKE IT FROM HERE...

Sometimes we are so blessed that we begin to think we're entitled to all the good things that come our way. Perhaps it's human nature. If you give a small child a gift, he'll treasure it. But if you give him two gifts, he'll might wonder why he didn't get a third.

What happens when you lose things you've come to expect? What happens when there's a power outage and you can't watch TV or operate your hair dryer? What happens when you get sick and can't do some of the things that you'd planned? If you're like most people, you probably become resentful and angry. You don't realize that the things you have are privileges, not rights. They are the blessings from God.

None of us deserves the things we have. We live very comfortably while people all over the world suffer. We take for granted things that other people have never experienced. Yet we still feel like we don't have enough. We want more. And we aren't very grateful for what we do have.

That's why it's important for us to practice an attitude of gratitude. We need to take time every day to thank God for the blessings he has given us (Colossians 3:15). When you're thankful for what you have, you'll be able to live every day with joy—whether you get more or not!

THE ECHO

ne day an angry little boy ran around his village shouting, "I hate you! I hate you!" No one knew quite how to respond to him.

Eventually the little boy ran to the edge of a steep cliff and shouted into the valley, "I hate you! I hate you!"

Back from the valley came an echo: "I hate you! I hate you!"

Startled at this, the boy ran home. With tears in his eyes, he told his mother that there was a mean little boy in the valley who shouted at him, "I hate you! I hate you!"

His mother took the boy back to the cliff and told him to shout, "I love you! I love you!"

When he did, back came the reply: "I love you! I love you!"

From that day on, the little boy wasn't angry anymore.

? WHERE TO TAKE IT FROM HERE...

Jesus said, "Give, and it will be given to you...for with the measure you use, it will be measured to you" (Luke 6:38). Paul put it this way: "Whoever sows sparingly will also reap sparingly, and whoever sows generously will also reap generously" (2 Corinthians 9:6).

This principle has withstood the test of time. What we do and say will come back to us like an echo. If we want to be treated with respect, we must learn to be respectful. If we want to have friends, we must learn to be friendly. Nobody owes you anything. You only get what you give.

BABOONS ON THE LOOSE

In eastern Africa a troop of about 50 baboons made themselves at home right next to a farm. The baboons were amusing at first but soon wore out their welcome. Before long they were ravaging the corn and other crops and helping themselves to anything they could get their hands on.

The frustrated farmers in the area made plans to have the animals destroyed. To do this they set up cages with food in them. Their plan was to capture the baboons and then kill them once they were trapped.

Baboons, however, aren't stupid animals. Sensing that the cages were dangerous, they refused to go in.

But the farmers were patient. After several days, one of the hungry baboons ventured into the cage and sampled the food. It was good—very good. And nothing bad happened.

The next day, the same baboon returned for more food. Other baboons soon followed. After a few days, the entire troop of baboons were going into the cages to feast on the food that had been put there by the farmers. Rather than being afraid of the cages, the baboons started to like them.

For several weeks, the baboons went into the cages every day to get their food. One day, however, the food was tied to the door latch. When the animals grabbed the food, the doors of the cages slammed shut.

The baboons were spooked at first, but quickly went back to finishing their meal. They showed no real concern for the fact they had been trapped in a cage.

? **WHERE TO TAKE IT FROM HERE...**

Sin is a lot like those baboon traps. Down deep you know it can harm you, but just like the food in those traps, it looks pretty good. And you're hungry! That's the sin nature.

You may try to resist temptation and do the right thing at first. But then you start to see other people indulging themselves without anything bad happening. And just like the baboons, you start to believe that you can get away with it yourself.

But the devil is very patient. He'll let you get away with sin for a while—maybe even a long time. Then he'll slam the door shut, and your life will be destroyed.

Fortunately, our story has a happy ending. The baboons didn't die. A wildlife biologist found out about the farmers' plan to destroy the baboons and rescued them. The foundation that supported the rescue effort actually paid the farmers for their losses and the expenses they incurred to trap the baboons. The baboons were then transported by truck to a remote location in the wild and set free.

In the same way, God sent his Son Jesus to rescue us from sin. We couldn't rescue ourselves, so Jesus came and paid the price for our salvation. "While we were still sinners, Christ died for us" (Romans 5:8). See also Colossians 1:13-14; 1 Thessalonians 1:9-10.

A LiTTLE PROBLEM

One day a little boy named Julian fell down while chasing butterflies in a field of tall grass. Soon afterward, the boy's left eye started hurting, so he was taken to a doctor. The doctor couldn't find the source of the irritation, so he just gave the boy some ointment and sent him home.

Eventually Julian's eye problem went away. About a year later, though, the boy started complaining of cloudy vision. His parents took him to an eye specialist, who was stunned by what he discovered.

Apparently when Julian had fallen a year earlier, a tiny grass seed had implanted itself in his cornea. Slowly the seed had grown and had actually sprouted two little leaves in Julian's eye. The seed had to be removed immediately in order to save the boy's vision.

? WHERE TO TAKE IT FROM HERE...

Sometimes when we fall into sin, we tell ourselves things like, "That didn't hurt."

But sin has a way of implanting itself into our hearts and growing into something that can do permanent damage to our souls. Sin can blur our vision and cause us to take our eyes off Christ. Satan wouldn't have it any other way.

Have you allowed sin to take root in your life? Is your vision blurred? Unless the root of sin is surgically removed, it will destroy you and your relationship with God. The removal can't be done with ointment. Only Jesus can get rid of your sin. That's why he went to the cross.

"If we confess our sins, he is faithful and just and will forgive us our sins and purify us from all unrighteousness" (1 John 1:9).

I Can Quit

Burt Hunter, a newspaper reporter and photographer in Long Beach, California, found himself on a strange mission one foggy morning. He was scheduled to interview and take pictures of a woman snake charmer.

When Burt visited the woman's home, he was surprised to find that she lived in a very nice, upper-class neighborhood. The woman herself didn't look someone who played with snakes. Burt couldn't help mentioning that fact to her.

"I don't understand why a wealthy, attractive woman such as yourself is engaged in this kind of business," he said. "It seems awfully dangerous to me."

The woman smiled and said, "Oh, I don't do it because I have to. It's a fascinating hobby. I really like the element of danger involved. Someday soon I plan to give it up and spend more time with my flowers. I can quit this any time I want to."

While Burt set up his equipment, the woman brought in baskets containing cobras. She confidently lifted some of the deadly snakes as he snapped pictures of her handling them.

After replacing the snakes in their baskets, she cautioned, "Be especially quiet now and don't make any quick moves. I'm going to take out my newest snake. It isn't completely used to me yet."

The woman lifted the new snake out of its basket, then suddenly stiffened. "Something's wrong," she whispered to the photographer. "I'm going to have to put him back." She opened the basket slowly and began to lower the snake into it.

With a lightning-fast jab, the cobra buried its fangs into the woman's wrist. The woman forced the snake into the basket and clutched her arm.

She spoke calmly to Burt, "Go quickly to my medicine chest and bring the snake serum. Hurry!" Trembling, Burt ran to the restroom and returned with the precious vial.

The woman instructed him to take out the syringe and fit the needle on. Then she told him how to withdraw the serum. Burt struggled with the unfamiliar task, his hands shaking badly. He braced his arm against the table as he tried desperately to get the needle into the vial. Suddenly he gasped. His clumsy fingers had crushed the tiny bottle. The serum, now useless, dripped through his fingers and onto the floor.

"Tell me," he urged. "Where can I get another?"

In a quiet voice she responded, "That was my last one."

The woman's agony ended when she died a few hours later. Burt's, however, continued for the rest of his life. He often recalled what the woman had said that day: "I can quit this anytime I want to."

 WHERE TO TAKE IT FROM HERE...

We all know people who are involved in behaviors that are just as dangerous as playing with poisonous snakes—people who say, "I can quit this any time I want to." But for some reason, they never do...until it's too late.

Satan is sometimes referred to in Scripture as a deadly snake. He first appeared in the Garden of Eden and persuaded Adam and Eve to commit the very first sins. And he didn't stop there. He still tempts us with sin, leading us to believe that it won't hurt us—that we can quit whenever we want.

But sin is very addictive. You may think you can let it go, but it won't let go of you. It may offer a thrill, a bit of excitement, or a momentary high, but it always leads to heartbreak and death (see Romans 6:23).

Are you playing around with sin? Give your life to Jesus, and let him change it. Only he can set you free from sin. Please do it now, because there will come a time when not even the serum of the Gospel can save you (see John 12:40). Your best opportunity to find freedom from the consequences of sin may be slipping through your fingers right now.

Who's Watching?

The 1964 Philadelphia Phillies will always be known as the team that suffered one of the great collapses in sports history. They let a huge division lead slip away by losing ten games in a row at the end of the season. Despite the collapse, the Phillies season had its share of memorable moments, including a perfect game and a ninth-inning home run by a Phillie to win the All-Star Game.

But the most remarkable moment of the entire season occurred after a game, not during it. Clay Dalrymple, a Phillie pitcher, was asked to assist a blind girl who had requested a chance to walk out on the field. Dalrymple took the girl to home plate where she reached down and felt the plate. Then they walked to first base, second base, and third base before ending up at home plate once again.

While Dalrymple was showing the girl around the bases, he never noticed that the fans remaining in the stadium had stopped to watch him and his companion. He just assumed that the silence in the stands meant the fans had gone home. But when the two of them finally reached home plate, the ballpark erupted. Dalrymple was shocked by the applause. When he looked up, he saw thousands of fans giving him a standing ovation.

Later, Dalrymple told a Sports Illustrated reporter, "It was the biggest ovation I ever got."

 WHERE TO TAKE IT FROM HERE...

Sometimes we forget that our efforts to be Christlike are observed by others—even though we may be unaware that they're watching. Remember, it's not the big things we do that matter, it's the right things we do.

Scripture tells us that we're surrounded by a "great cloud of witnesses." That's why we should "run with perseverance the race marked out for us" (Hebrews 12:1). We should act like Jesus even when we don't think anyone is watching. At the very least, the angels in heaven are cheering us on (Luke 15:10).

Sobibor

The Sobibor Nazi concentration camp was set in the scenic woods near the Bug River, which separates Poland and Russia. The natural beauty of the setting stood in stark contrast to the stench and horror of the camp, where torture and death awaited every man, woman, and child who arrived there.

On October 14, 1943, Jewish slave laborers in Sobibor surprised their captors by using their shovels and pickaxes as weapons in a well-planned attack. Some of the Jewish prisoners cut the electricity to the fence and used captured pistols and rifles to shoot their way past the German guards. Hundreds of others stormed through the barbed wire and mine fields to the potential safety of the nearby forest.

Of the 700 prisoners who took part in the escape, 300 made it to the forest. Of those, less than 100 are known to have survived. Most were hunted down by the Germans and executed.

One of the former prisoners who lived to talk about Sobibor was a man named Thomas Blatt—or Toivi, as he was known in his native Poland. Toivi was 15 years old when his family was herded into Sobibor. His parents were executed in the gas chamber, but Toivi, who was young and healthy, was a prime candidate for slave labor.

In the confusion of the escape, Toivi had attempted to crawl through a hole in the barbed wire fence but was trampled by the prisoners who stormed the fence and ran through the minefield. As a result, Toivi was one of the last to escape the camp.

Toivi and two companions started their long journey through the dense woods. Every morning at daybreak they buried themselves in the woods to sleep. Every night they made their way through the trees and thick brush. The boys had much to drive them on—vigor, youth, determination, revenge, fear, and a deep desire to survive. Most significantly, they had regained something they'd once lost—hope.

But what they really needed was a guide—someone who could read the stars, someone who knew north from south and east from west. All three of them were city boys with few outdoors skills.

After four nights of wandering through the cold forest, the three boys saw a building silhouetted against the dark sky in the distance. With smiles on their faces, they eagerly approached it with the hope that it might provide sanctuary from their enemies.

As they got closer, they noticed that the building they had seen was a tower—specifically, the east tower of the Sobibor concentration camp!

They had made one giant circle through the woods and ended up exactly where they started.

Terrified, the three boys plunged back into the forest. But only Toivi lived to tell about their awful experience.

 WHERE TO TAKE IT FROM HERE...

Many people in today's world work tirelessly to escape from a life without meaning, only to find themselves traveling in circles. They pursue pleasure, prestige, or possessions, and more often than not find themselves right back where they started—in a prison of meaninglessness that denies them hope and freedom.

"There is a way that seems right to a man, but in the end it leads to death" (Proverbs 16:25).

But there is good news. An escape route exists, and Jesus wants to guide us to it (Matthew 7:14). That's why he came—to show us the way that leads to life.

"Then Jesus said to his disciples, 'If anyone would come after me, he must deny himself and take up his cross and follow me'" (Matthew 16:24).

Let Jesus be your guide.

LASHED to THE MAST

The Odyssey, an epic Greek poem, tells the story of King Odysseus and his heroic struggle against the gods. The tale begins when the ship of Odysseus is blown off course on the way home from the Trojan Wars. In his effort to get home, Odysseus lands on an island where he encounters one-eyed monsters known as Cyclops.

One of the Cyclops, Polyphemus, captures the humans and begins devouring them. Odysseus, in order to save himself and his crew, blinds the eye of the giant and manages to escape from the island.

What Odysseus doesn't know is that Polyphemus, the Cyclops he blinded, is the son of the Greek god Poseidon. In retaliation, Poseidon tries to prevent Odysseus from ever reaching home.

To accomplish his goal, Poseidon places Odysseus's ship in the path of the Island of Sirens. The island is inhabited by beautiful women (sirens) who sing out to sailors on the sea, enticing them to steer their ships to destruction on the jagged reefs that surround the island. The sirens' songs could be heard for great distances.

As Odysseus sails for home, he can hear the songs of the sirens. He's also well aware of his vulnerability to their seductive power. His solution is to lash himself to his ship's mast so he can listen to their songs but not respond to them. The rest of the crew stuffs their ears to block the sound.

In agony, Odysseus remains lashed to the mast until his ship makes it safely past the island. As a result, he manages to stay on course until he arrives home safely.

 WHERE TO TAKE IT FROM HERE...

As we sail the sea of life, we will encounter many temptations and entice-ments that will threaten to take us off course and destroy us. The Bible tells us that Satan "prowls around like a roaring lion, looking for someone to devour" (1 Peter 5:8)—not unlike Poseidon in The Odyssey.

Our best strategy for defeating Satan is not necessarily to withdraw from the world so that we can't hear his songs. Instead, we must remain "lashed to the mast"—the cross of Jesus Christ. Our calling as Christians is to be "in the world, but not of it." We should be involved in the world without allowing its seductive power to undermine our integrity. We must remain faithful to who we are as Christians and to resist temptation.

We do this by intentionally tying ourselves to the church, to other Christians, to the Word of God, and to the disciplines of the Christian life. So if you don't take steps to insure your survival, you will always be in grave danger. "If you think you are standing firm, be careful that you don't fall!" (1 Corinthians 10:12).

Alyssa

All through high school, Alyssa tried to share her faith in Christ with her four closest friends. In long late-night conversations, they'd talk about everything from heaven to abortion to the existence of evil in the world. Alyssa loved her friends and wanted them to know Christ the way she did.

After they graduated, the four friends tried to stay in touch. Even though they moved to different parts of the country, they e-mailed each other, got together at holidays, and even took vacations together during the summer. Sometimes they'd have conversations like the ones of old, with Alyssa talking about her beliefs and her relationship with God.

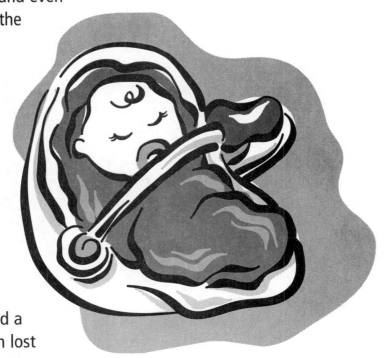

While Alyssa's friends always treated her with respect, they never became Christians. Their decision—or, rather, their lack of a decision—was a real disappointment to Alyssa.

After college Alyssa accepted a job across the country and soon lost touch with her friends. When she came back home for Christmas one year, she ran into one of them at a local department store.

Her friend was pushing a baby stroller and proudly introduced her new baby to Alyssa. When Alyssa found out that her friend wasn't married, she thought, *A lot of good all that talking about God did. Look what happened to her. She ended up getting pregnant before she got married.*

Toward the end of their conversation, Alyssa asked if she could hold the baby. As her friend handed the infant to her, she said, "You know, Alyssa, you're partly to thank for this baby. If it wasn't for you, I would have had an abortion. But I kept remembering all we had talked about and just couldn't do it."

WHERE TO TAKE IT FROM HERE...

You may not think your witness for Christ does any good, but it does. Obviously your ultimate hope is that your friends will come to know the Lord; however, that's not the only result that can come from being a witness. You never know how God will use what you do for him. Even when you can't see the results of your obedience, you can trust that God will take what you do and use it to bear fruit.

WAYWARD SONS

A Jewish man named Levi was troubled by the life his son had chosen, and he went to see his old friend Mordecai about it.

"Mordecai," he said, "I brought my son up in the Jewish faith, gave him a very expensive bar mitzvah, and paid a fortune to educate him. Then he tells me last week he's decided to be a Christian. Where did I go wrong?"

"Funny you should come to me," said Mordecai. "I too brought my boy up in the faith, sent him to the best schools at great expense, only to find that he converted to the Christian faith. I have been in great turmoil over this."

The two men decided to ask their rabbi for advice.

"Funny you should come to me," said the rabbi after hearing the men's stories. "Like you two, I brought my boy up in the faith and put him through the university, which cost me a fortune. Then one day he too tells me he has decided to become a Christian."

"And what did you do?" the men asked.

"I turned to God for the answer" replied the rabbi.

"And what did He say?" the two men questioned.

"He said, 'Funny you should come to me...'"

? WHERE TO TAKE IT FROM HERE...

The apostle Paul wrote, "Brothers, my heart's desire and prayer to God for the Israelites is that they may be saved...Christ is the end of the law so that there may be righteousness for everyone who believes" (Romans 10:1, 4).

The good news of the gospel is for everyone. "The same Lord is Lord of all and richly blesses all who call on him, for, everyone who calls on the name of the Lord will be saved" (Romans 10:12-13).

In our age of political correctness, we sometimes tend to avoid telling people about Jesus because we don't want to offend them. We may have been led to believe that there are many paths to God and that no one religion is better than any other. But while it is important always to treat others with respect, the Bible does not support the claim that there are many paths to God. Jesus himself said, "No one comes to the Father except through me" (John 14:6).

Paul continues in Romans 10 by writing, "How, then, can they call on the one they have not believed in? And how can they believe in the one of whom they have not heard? And how can they hear without someone preaching to them?" (10:14). It is the responsibility of every Christian to tell everyone we meet about Jesus, the only way to God.

You're Not a Monk

A traveler's car broke down near a monastery late one night. With no place else to go, he walked to the monastery and explained his situation. The monks graciously invited him to spend the night, gave him something warm to drink, and even repaired his car.

During the night, the man heard a strange sound. The next morning, he asked the monks about it.

"We can't tell you, you're not a monk," they replied.

The man was disappointed, but thanked them for their hospitality and went on his way.

Some years later, the same traveler had car problems in front of the same monastery. Once again, the monks were happy to give him a place to stay, feed him, and fix his car.

And during the night, he heard the same strange noise that he had heard years earlier.

The next morning, he asked again, "What was that noise I heard during the night?"

The monks replied, "We can't tell you, you're not a monk."

The traveler said, "All these years I've wondered about that sound. I'm dying to know what it is. So how do I become a monk?"

The monks explained, "First, you must travel the earth and learn to speak the language of every culture and tribe that exists in the world. Then you must do one kind deed for every man, woman, and child on the planet. Finally, you must climb to the top of the highest mountain and count the number of stars that exist in the heavens. When you have done all this, you will be well on your way toward becoming a monk."

Undaunted, the man accepted the task. Some forty-five years later, he returned to the monastery and knocked on the door. "I have traveled the earth and learned more than six thousand languages. I have performed kind deeds for nine billion people. I almost froze to death on the highest mountain, where I learned that there are more than 17 trillion stars."

The monks were amazed. "Congratulations," they said. "you are very close to being a monk of the highest order. We shall now take you to the source of the sound."

They led the man to a wooden door, where one of the monks said, "The sound is right behind that door."

The man tried to open the door, but it was locked.

"How do I open it?" he asked.

"You must first memorize the Old Testament," the monks told him.

The man went to his room and, in a matter of just a few months, memorized the entire Old Testament. In return, he was given the key to the wooden door and taken back to it.

Upon opening the door, he encountered another door made of brass. It was locked. "To receive the key that will open the brass door," the monks said, "you must memorize the New Testament."

Frustrated, the man went back to his room and memorized the New Testament. Within a few months, he had the key to the brass door. Again the monks accompanied him to the source of the strange sound.

Inside the brass door was yet another door, this one made of gold. It too was locked. The monks said, "This is the last door. But to receive the key, you must spend one year in the dungeon, with only bread and water to sustain you."

The man endured his year in the dungeon. Emaciated and weary, he was once again taken to the source of the sound. He unlocked the wooden door and the brass door. Then the monks gave him the key to the gold door.

With trembling hands, the man unlocked the door, turned the knob, and opened it. Behind it lay the source of the sound—and, without a doubt, it was worth all those years of suffering and pain.

Want to know what it was?

Sorry, I can't tell you. You're not a monk.

WHERE TO TAKE IT FROM HERE...

It's frustrating when people withhold information from us. We want to know everything. Unfortunately, some things will remain a mystery. For example, we don't always know why God does what he does or why things happen that we can't explain. The Bible describes it as seeing "through a glass, darkly" (1 Corinthians 13:12, KJV).

The good news is that our questions will be answered in heaven. We just have to be patient.

The better news is that you don't have to be a monk to get into heaven. You don't have to jump through impossible hoops. If you know Jesus and trust him as your Savior, you have the key.

In the meantime, we must trust God and have confidence that, even though we don't have all the answers, he does.

Only a Prayer

Don't ever tell John "Tex" Teixeria that prayer doesn't work.

Tex spent his life as a fisherman in the channels of the Hawaiian Islands. On a deceptively calm night in 1967, Tex guided his 40-foot fishing boat toward the beach of an otherwise inaccessible canyon on the north side of Molokai. He had agreed to allow some friends to go ashore, using the fishing vessel's small skiff, for some wild pig hunting while he and the rest of the crew did some night fishing.

Returning to the rendezvous spot early the next morning, the men found that conditions had changed. Huge waves ripped through the channel and crashed into the boat, nearly capsizing it and (unbeknownst to the crew) fatally weakening it.

The fate of the small skiff full of hunters waiting on the shoreline was immediately apparent. Its bottom had been torn off by the rugged lava rocks.

With great difficulty, a tow line was brought to the shivering hunters who, while holding on to inflated plastic tarps and an ice chest filled with their kill, were dragged by the boat's winch through the surf to the vessel. When all the men were safely on board, the huge craft gunned away from the island.

Exhausted after fishing all night and the adventure of the morning, Tex went below deck to sleep. A few hours later he was awakened by his panicked friends. The boat was sinking.

By the time Tex got to the deck, there was nothing he could do except order everyone into the water. Without the skiff, the eight men on board the fishing vessel had only life jackets and inner tubes to keep them afloat.

Bobbing in the water, Tex remembered the ice chests full of freshly slaughtered game and fish. He knew that sharks would be in the area within minutes, so he encouraged the men to paddle as fast as they could away from the sunken boat.

All eight of the men knew they were in big trouble. The currents in the channel were sweeping them into the open ocean. But as night

approached it seemed that their salvation was near. Bouncing up and down in the inky sea, the men thought they could make out the lights of a boat in the distance. Two of the men decided to swim toward the lights.

It turned out that they weren't boat lights at all. They were the airplane warning lights on the top of Koko Head, a far-distant mountain.

The two men were never seen again.

By morning the situation had worsened. One of the inner tubes was losing air. The men had no food or water. The planes that passed overhead could not see them bobbing in the middle of the Pacific.

It was then that Tex decided to call a prayer meeting. No one objected. With all hope gone, the group of tough, self-sufficient sailors had only one place to turn. They huddled together in their life jackets and inner tubes and, with loud cries, pleaded for God to intervene.

The moment the last man finished his prayer, Tex looked up. "A stick!" he cried out.

The stick was standing vertically out of the water. It appeared to be a fishing buoy or a marker of some kind. If they could get to it, Tex reasoned, someone might come along to check it and find them. At the very least, it might support the ones who were losing air in their inner tubes. Using all of their energy to fight the current, the men paddled toward the stick.

Suddenly the stick began to move rapidly in their direction. The six men stopped paddling, stunned and puzzled.

Seconds later there was an incredible whoosh that seemed to pull the ocean out from under them. At the same moment, a monster emerged from the depths.

It was a nuclear submarine.

The hatch opened and the captain of the sub came to the observation deck as the men in the ocean screamed wildly.

They had been rescued.

Huddled below deck and nursing hot coffee, the six tired survivors listened awestruck as the captain explained that it was against orders for him to surface his sub anywhere outside of Pearl Harbor and that he expected to face disciplinary action for what he had done.

"But," he explained softly, "something beyond my control told me to go to the surface. I can't explain it. Something just told me to bring the sub up, right then and there. I did...and there you were."

 **WHERE TO TAKE IT FROM HERE...**

This true story is just one example of how God answers prayer. On occasion, God's intervention in our lives is obvious and spectacular. At other times, however, he works quietly in our lives and asks us to trust that he has everything under control—even when things don't work out the way we expected.

We can be confident that God is faithful. He hears and answers when we pray. "Ask and you will receive, and your joy will be made complete" (John 16:24).

God's Pictures

Sally walked to and from school every day. She loved skipping along the sidewalk, looking at the flowers, and saying hi to neighbors and shopkeepers along the way.

One morning, the sky was cloudy and rain was forecast for later in the day. But Sally still wanted to walk to school. Her mother allowed her to but told her to take her umbrella, just in case.

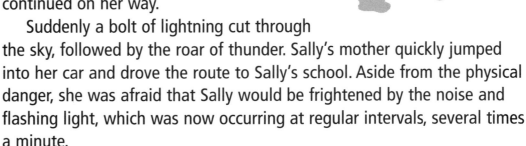

When school was over, Sally began her walk home. As she skipped along, the wind began to howl and raindrops started falling from the sky. Sally opened her umbrella and continued on her way.

Suddenly a bolt of lightning cut through the sky, followed by the roar of thunder. Sally's mother quickly jumped into her car and drove the route to Sally's school. Aside from the physical danger, she was afraid that Sally would be frightened by the noise and flashing light, which was now occurring at regular intervals, several times a minute.

Around the corner, Sally's mother saw her little girl walking along with her umbrella. But at each flash of lightning, Sally would stop, look up at the sky, and smile.

Sally's mother watched this routine repeat itself three times. Each lightning flash caused Sally to stop walking, look up at the sky, and smile. Finally, Sally's mother called to her, "Sally, what on earth are you doing?"

Sally answered, "I'm smiling. God keeps taking pictures of me."

WHERE TO TAKE IT FROM HERE...

It's been said that if God has a wallet, you can bet your picture is in it. The next time you're in a storm of life, remember that God may just be snapping a few pictures of you! Smile!

Bored and Busy

A local newspaper had a Sunday morning religion section that contained, among other things, letters to the editor about various religious issues. Most weeks these letters were pretty innocuous, but one Sunday something was printed that became quite controversial.

A man wrote:

> I quit going to church this year. I decided that listening to sermons week after week was a stupid thing to do. After all, I went to church for more than 40 years and during my lifetime I probably heard 5,000 sermons. I can only remember about five of them. What a waste of time.
>
> —Bored and Busy

This sparked a fury of incoming letters. Some people wrote that sermons do make a difference, while others sided with Bored and Busy's opinion that they were basically meaningless and unnecessary. Finally, one letter was printed that ended the debate:

> I quit eating this year. Thanks to Bored and Busy's insights, I decided that eating week after week was a stupid thing to do. After all, I have been eating for more than 40 years and during my lifetime I probably have eaten 5,000 meals. I can only remember about five of them. What a waste of time.
>
> —Starved and Stupid

 WHERE TO TAKE IT FROM HERE...

Sometimes you may wonder what good it does to listen to sermons or participate in weekly Bible studies or have daily devotions. Like the first letter writer in the story, you may feel that you're too bored or busy for the things of God. But don't overlook the fact that you need those things to survive.

In order to grow as a Christian, you need spiritual food (1 Corinthians 3:2). You need to feed on the Word of God. Not every spiritual meal is going to be memorable, but it will provide you with the nourishment you need to survive and thrive as a Christian.

Too Late

A surgeon was awakened by a phone call at 2:30 one frigid winter morning. The nurse on the line explained that an eight-year-old boy had been hit by a car and was bleeding profusely. The attending physician had determined that unless the boy was operated on immediately, he would not survive.

The surgeon threw on his clothes and rushed out into the subzero weather. He scraped his car's windshield just enough to be able to see where he was going and started the icy five-mile trip to the hospital. Each time he stopped at a red light he opened his car door and leaned out just enough to scrape a little more ice from the windshield.

At one intersection, about a mile and a half from the hospital, the surgeon noticed a man wearing a brown coat and an old green hat impatiently trying to cross the street. As the surgeon leaned out of his car, the man rushed over, grabbed him by his coat, and pulled him to the ground.

The surgeon tried to put up a fight but was no match for the burly, and apparently desperate, man. While the surgeon struggled to his feet, the man jumped in the surgeon's car and drove away.

Unhurt, the surgeon hurried to a phone booth and called for a cab. Twenty minutes later he finally made it to the hospital.

"Where's the boy who was hit by a car?" he asked one of the nurses as he hurried through the emergency room.

The nurse's eyes welled up with tears. "We couldn't stop the bleeding," she said. "He died just a few minutes ago. His parents are still in the waiting area, if you'd like to speak to them."

The surgeon took a deep breath and walked out into the waiting area. A woman in a long red coat was sitting in the middle of the room, sobbing silently into her hands. Behind her, a man stood with his hand on her shoulder. His head was bowed and his eyes were closed.

He was wearing a brown coat and an old green hat.

The boy's father, in his rush to get to the hospital, had pushed aside the one man who could have saved his son's life. How many people rush through life pushing aside the Great Physician—the only one who is capable of giving them life?

Jesus alone can bring healing and hope to broken lives, broken families, and broken relationships. It's our job to make sure the world knows who he is so they can receive him rather than turn him away.

"How then, can they call on the name of the one they have not believed in? And how can they believe in the one of whom they have not heard?...How beautiful are the feet of those who bring good news!" (Romans 10:14-15).

Let There Be Peace

"Those kids will drive you crazy!"

That's what the old man's friends told him when he bought the small, well-kept house just down the street from the local junior high school. Contrary to their warnings though, the man's first few weeks in his new house went without a hitch.

Then the new school year began.

The very next afternoon three young boys, full of pent-up energy, whooped their way down his street, beating merrily on every trash can they passed. The crashing percussion continued day after day, until finally the man decided it was time to take some action.

One afternoon he walked out to meet the young percussionists as they banged their way home. He said, "You kids are a lot of fun. I like to see you express your excitement like that because it reminds me of the things I used to do when I was your age. In fact, I like it so much that I'll give you each a dollar if you'll promise to come around every day and do your thing." The kids grinned at each other and agreed to continue their afternoon trash can performances.

After a few days, the old-timer greeted the kids again, but this time he had a sad smile on his face. "This recession's really putting a big dent in my income," he told them. "From now on, I'll only be able to pay you 50 cents to beat on the trash cans."

The noisemakers were obviously disappointed, but they accepted his offer and continued their daily ruckus. A few days later, the wily retiree approached the kids again as they drummed their way down the street.

"Look," he said, "I haven't received my Social Security check yet, so I'm not going to be able to give you more than 25 cents. Will that be okay?"

"A lousy quarter?" the drum leader exclaimed. "If you think we're going to waste our time beating these cans around for a quarter, you're nuts! No way, mister. We quit!"

And from that day on, the old man enjoyed peace in the afternoon.

By turning the drummers' fun into work, the wise old man was able to sap the enjoyment from what they were doing. Sometimes the devil tries to trick Christians in the same way. If he sees us serving God out of pure enjoyment and love, he may try to focus our attention on the rewards we stand to gain instead. Whether it's status, recognition, fame, glory, or even a better "mansion in heaven," if the devil can get us thinking about selfish motives for serving God, there's a good chance he can sap the carefree joy that comes from doing what we were created to do.

WHAT CHAIR?

Several years ago at a prestigious university, a philosophy professor gave his students a one-question final exam. He picked up a chair, placed it on top of his desk, and wrote on the board, "Using what you have learned in class this semester, prove that this chair does not exist."

Most of the students dug deep and wrote like crazy for the entire hour. Some of them churned out more than 30 pages of heady philosophical debate and logic.

One student, though, handed in his paper after less than a minute. As it turned out, he was the only one in the class who got an "A" on the test.

His answer consisted of two words: "What chair?"

? WHERE TO TAKE IT FROM HERE...

Most atheists who believe they can disprove the existence of God using their philosophical and reasoning skills often unwittingly end up acknowledging his existence. God has made himself known in his creation and revealed himself in the lives of his people, leaving the atheist with the formidable task of trying to disprove the obvious.

The story is told of an atheist who said to a believer, "I don't believe God exists." The believer thought for a minute and said, "Well, I don't think God believes you exist, either." The atheist blurted out, "What do you mean! He has to believe I exist because he created me!"

The Bus Driver's Gift

One afternoon a bus driver was taking 40 children home from school. As the bus made its way down a steep grade, the brakes failed. The driver was unable to steer the bus to the left because of a high embankment or to the right because of a steep cliff.

As the bus hurtled down the hill, the driver recalled that there was a narrow gate at the bottom which led into a field. He decided to try to steer the bus through the gate and into the field, figuring that it would eventually come to a safe stop. He hoped that no cars or other obstacles would get in his way before he got to the gate.

When the bus reached the bottom of the hill, the driver saw the gate approaching fast. But to his horror, he noticed a small child sitting on the gate, waving at the bus.

It was too late to change plans now. If the driver tried to avoid the gate, 40 children would die. He cried out in anguish as the bus slammed directly into the gate. The innocent child died instantly in the collision, but the bus and all of its passengers were saved.

Emergency vehicles were the first to arrive on the scene, followed shortly by relieved parents and grandparents. Many of them wanted to show their appreciation and gratitude to the driver who had kept the bus under control long enough to save their children. But the driver was nowhere to be found. They asked a police officer where he had gone.

"They've taken him to the hospital," the officer said. "He's suffering from severe shock."

"Well, that's understandable," they replied.

"No, you don't understand," said the officer. "You see, that little boy on the fence was his own son."

? WHERE TO TAKE IT FROM HERE...

God's decision to save us came at a great expense to himself. Jesus cried out in the garden, "My Father, if it is possible, may this cup be taken from me" (Matthew 26:39). But it was God's love for us that sent Jesus to the cross (John 3:16). He gave his only son so that we could live.

E-FLAT

rturo Toscanini, the great conductor, was sitting at his podium before a concert one evening. As the orchestra warmed up just minutes before the performance, a bassoon player approached him in a fearful panic. "Maestro, I am very sorry, but my instrument has suffered an accident, and the E-flat will not sound. I am afraid I will not be able to play tonight."

Upon hearing this news, Toscanini went silent and closed his eyes. The bassoon player cowered in fear of his fury. The great conductor put his hands to his head and continued in silence, adding to the poor bassoon player's agony.

At last Toscanini looked up and said quietly, "Do not worry. E-flat does not appear in your music tonight." Toscanini had played through the entire concert in his mind, reviewing every note the bassoon player would have to play. With his intimate knowledge of the music, the conductor was able to reassure the bassoon player that everything would be all right.

? WHERE TO TAKE IT FROM HERE...

Do you ever wonder about the future and what it might hold for you? Do you ever wonder whether you have what it takes to succeed, to do something important with your life?

God knows the future. He has looked ahead at the score of your life and has good news for you. "'For I know the plans I have for you,' declares the Lord, 'plans to prosper you and not to harm you, plans to give you hope and a future'"(Jeremiah 29:11). God has given you everything you need play your part in his grand symphony. Pick up your bassoon and start making music!

Not a Good Example

A rather pompous, self-righteous Sunday School teacher was trying to make the point that good Christians don't keep their faith a secret. With her head held high and her chest thrust out, the teacher strutted impressively back and forth across the room. She asked, "Now, class, why do you think people call me a Christian?"

The room was silent for a moment. Then one of the boys slowly raised his hand and said, "Probably because they don't know you."

 WHERE TO TAKE IT FROM HERE...

Witnessing for Christ first means living for Christ. You don't have to be a great leader to bring others to Christ. You just have to be a great follower—a disciple of Christ.

Jesus criticized the Pharisees for saying one thing and doing another. Like that Sunday School teacher, they were pompous and self-righteous. They wore their religious titles proudly on their sleeves, as if that was enough to get them into heaven.

While other people may not have known what the Pharisees were really like, Jesus sure did. He could see their hearts, and he called them "whitewashed tombs" (Matthew 23:27). The Pharisees were hypocrites.

Jesus wants us to demonstrate humility and not to think of ourselves more highly than we ought to think (Romans 12:3). If we confess that we're sinners in need of a Savior, and treat others with dignity and respect, we will do more to communicate Christ than all the sermons in the world.

HEP Baddy

The weather was perfect—a day made for raking leaves. With his trusty rake, the man began gathering the leaves into tidy piles. Once they were in piles, he planned to bag them and haul them to the curb. He figured he could get the job done in about an hour.

Just as the man finished his third pile, his two-year-old son Justin came charging out of the house. The excited boy was shouting, "Hep baddy! Hep baddy!" at the top of his lungs. Holding a small plastic rake, he ran toward his baddy to hep rake up the leaves.

Justin's father was excited about his son's enthusiasm, but he knew the little guy probably wouldn't be much hep. Still, he smiled at his son and said, "Why, thank you, Justin! I really do need your help!"

As the man began raking a fourth pile, he noticed Justin working on pile number three. The little boy swung his rake vigorously at the leaves, sending them flying everywhere. All the while he repeated the words, "Hep baddy! Hep baddy!"

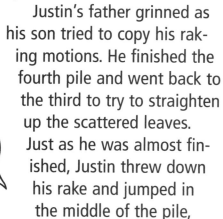

Justin's father grinned as his son tried to copy his raking motions. He finished the fourth pile and went back to the third to try to straighten up the scattered leaves. Just as he was almost finished, Justin threw down his rake and jumped in the middle of the pile, still shouting, "Hep baddy! Hey baddy!" He buried himself in the pile, laughing and kicking his legs, scattering leaves everywhere.

This went on for several hours. The man would rake a pile and the boy would mess it up. When it came time to put the leaves into bags, Justin wanted to help with that, too. Again his father graciously allowed him to participate, even though the job could have been completed a whole lot quicker—and certainly a whole lot better—if the father had done it himself.

Unfortunately some dads don't realize that bonding time with a child is more important than a great-looking lawn. They don't understand that it's more important to give a youngster a sense of importance and accomplishment than it is to complete a job early enough to catch the afternoon football game on TV.

Our heavenly Father doesn't need our help, but he loves us deeply. Certainly he's capable of getting things done in the world much faster and better than we can. However, he graciously allows us to be part of the process. He invites us to "hep baddy" by throwing ourselves into ministry and service to him. Even though we are apt to make a giant mess of things, he urges us on.

Remember Moses? God certainly could have rescued the Hebrew children without Moses' help. But God used Moses and assured him, "I will be with you" (Exodus 3:12)—and he most definitely was.

God also will be with you as you serve him. You may mess up big time, but he loves you and knows that he can always make things okay, if necessary. He wants to be with you, and he wants you to experience the joy of serving him!

Saved by Stirrups

When you think of the great inventions of humankind, you probably think of the wheel, the printing press, or the computer. You probably don't think of the stirrup.

While history books contain several accounts of how and when stirrups were invented, this version demonstrates the great impact stirrups had on human history.

In the year 1066, Edward the Confessor died, leaving no heir to the throne of England. Harold, Earl of Wessex, immediately took the throne for himself and held it for a tumultuous four weeks until William, Duke of Normandy, invaded England to take it from him. The fight that ensued became known as the Battle of Hastings.

When the English and Norman armies met at Hastings, their forces were evenly matched. But it was William's invention of the stirrup that turned the tide of battle in his favor.

Horses had long been a part of Middle Age military strategy, but their roles had been limited to that of support and transport. When the English arrived at Hastings, they came on horseback; when they prepared for battle, they sent the horses to the rear. Experience had taught them that an armored knight on horseback was too easily toppled in battle. Without a horse, a knight was harmless and vulnerable. The English, therefore, prepared to engage their enemy in the traditional style of warfare—hand-to-hand combat.

William began the battle with an artillery barrage from his archers and then charged with his infantry. When the English defenses held firm, William unveiled his secret weapon—mounted knights whose feet were secured to their horses with stirrups. From that secure platform, the knights were able to fight with a force previously unknown in military history. The English army was routed, and Harold was killed. Duke William of Normandy became William I, king of England, better known today as William the Conqueror.

As a result of William's conquest, England rose to influence and power and gave birth to many of the advances of Western civilization, including the United States of America.

 ## WHERE TO TAKE IT FROM HERE...

Christians are also engaged in a battle. As the apostle Paul described it, "For our struggle is not against flesh and blood, but against the rulers, against the authorities, against the powers of this dark world and against the spiritual forces of evil in the heavenly realms" (Ephesians 6:12).

That's a pretty scary description of the enemy. It's no wonder many Christians, like the knights of old, risk being toppled in battle.

But God has given us an advantage over the enemy. He has given us a stirrup in the person of the Holy Spirit. The Holy Spirit's presence in our lives enables us to fight against the powers of evil with a force that was previously unknown (Acts 1:8).

Just as the advantage of the stirrup helped William to become known as "the Conqueror," so we have the powerful advantage of the Holy Spirit to help us become "more than conquerors" in Christ Jesus (Romans 8:37).

I Know You

The whole town had gathered in the courthouse for the trial. The prosecuting attorney called his first witness, an elderly woman, to the stand. He approached her and asked, "Mrs. Jones, do you know me?"

She responded, "Why, yes, I do know you, Mr. Williams. I've known you since you were a young boy. And, frankly, you've been a big disappointment to me. You lie, you cheat on your wife, you manipulate people and talk about them behind their backs. You think you're a rising big shot, but you haven't the brains to realize you will never amount to anything more than a two-bit paper pusher. Yes, I know you."

The lawyer was stunned. Not knowing what else to do, he pointed across the room and asked, "Mrs. Jones, do you know the defense attorney?"

She replied, "Why, of course I do. I've known Mr. Bradley since he was a youngster, too. I used to baby-sit him. And he, too, has been a real disappointment to me. He's lazy, bigoted, and has a drinking problem. The man can't build a normal relationship with anyone, and his law practice is one of the shoddiest in the entire state. Yes, I know him."

At this point, the judge rapped the courtroom to silence and called both counselors to the bench.

In a very quiet voice, he said with menace, "If either of you ask her if she knows me, I'll hold you both in contempt of court!"

? WHERE TO TAKE IT FROM HERE...

Many of us go to great lengths to hide the truth about ourselves. We live behind all kinds of masks that conceal who we really are. We buy into the philosophy that image is everything.

Why do we do this? In most cases, it's because we're afraid of rejection. We don't think people will like us if they know anything about our past, our failures, our inadequacies, or our problems. So we do everything we can to look cool, successful, or happy—when, in reality, we are none of those things.

Keep in mind that the people who love you the most are those who know you the best. Most parents are a good example of that. You may hide a lot from them, but they know you pretty well. They've been there when you messed up again and again—yet they keep right on loving you.

God knows more about you than even your parents know. In fact, he knows more about you than you know about you (Psalm 139). Yet he loves you more than you will ever know.

Does God just ignore your past? No, but he can forgive it. And when he forgives, he forgets. That doesn't mean he doesn't know what you've done; it just means that he no longer holds what you've done against you. Your sins are blotted out, removed from your life's résumé "as far as the east is from the west" (Psalm 103:12).

In the story, the judge was afraid to hear what that woman might say about him. But we don't have to be afraid to hear what God has to say about us. If we have received forgiveness for our sins through faith in Christ, he has nothing but good things to say! Draw near to him and listen to his voice.

IT'S THE WATER

The islands around Indonesia are among the most beautiful in the world—crystalline tropical water, beautiful reefs with fish colored in every hue of the rainbow, powerful waves, and tranquil bays.

Tourists, surfers, and scuba divers from around the world have discovered these hidden jewels and pay large sums of money to enjoy this unspoiled aquatic playground.

But many of the locals won't swim. Neither will they dive, surf, wade, bathe, or do anything else that places their bodies in the warm, inviting water. Their fear of the water is so powerful that even though they are surrounded by ocean and must sail out in fishing boats for their daily sustenance, hardly any of the islanders ever learned to swim.

Why do they deny themselves the pleasure of exploring the natural wonders all around them? Because a long time ago, someone told them a lie. Someone told them that the ocean was full of demons and that swimming in it would bring harm to themselves and their families. And many Indonesian islanders still believe it.

 WHERE TO TAKE IT FROM HERE...

Just as for centuries those island people have missed out on the joy of frolicking in the surf and exploring their underwater world, so there are many people today who are missing out on the joy of knowing Christ and walking in fellowship with God. They believe that God is some kind of cosmic killjoy who wants to take away their fun and make their lives dull, boring, and utterly miserable.

Nothing could be further from the truth. "Though you have not seen him, you love him; and even though you do not see him now, you believe in him and are filled with an inexpressible and glorious joy" (1 Peter 1:8). Jesus came to give the best life possible, life "to the full" (John 10:10). Don't believe those who want to deprive you of that.

Looking for Jesus

One Sunday morning nine-year-old Joshua decided to skip church and go for a long walk. His mother frequently told him that if he skipped church, he would miss a chance to see Jesus. But Joshua had been going to church his whole life and had never seen Jesus there before, so he didn't think he'd be missing much. Besides, his church was an old, small, run-down building—just a little too confining for his desire to run and play.

Joshua's walk took him across the railroad tracks in town for the first time in his life. He noticed that the houses on the other side of the tracks were much bigger and much nicer than any in the poor neighborhood where he lived.

A few blocks later Joshua found himself in front of the biggest, most beautiful church he had ever seen. The steeple alone seemed as tall as a mountain. As he got closer, the big church bells stopped ringing and the last people filed in from the parking lot. They all had nice cars and wore nice clothes. He didn't see any people from his side of the tracks going to this church.

"This must be the church where Jesus goes," Joshua told himself. "It's so big and nice." As he walked closer, he could hear the music coming from inside. He remembered hearing his mother talk about how angels sing to Jesus in heaven. "Wow!" said Joshua as he listened to the choir. "I'll bet those are angels singing to Jesus!"

He walked up the steps, through the big front doors, and into the spacious lobby. He continued through another set of doors and entered the sanctuary. It was the biggest room he had ever seen. "This must be where Jesus is!" Joshua whispered to himself.

He noticed an empty seat a few rows from the back, so he sat down to scan the crowd, so he could find Jesus. The choir stopped singing and a large man in a black suit tapped Joshua on the shoulder. The man leaned down and asked Joshua if he could speak with him outside.

In the lobby, the man asked, "Son, where do you live?"

Joshua answered, "Well, if you go down the hill, take a left at the

corner, cross the railroad tracks, and head down that street a few more blocks, that's where I live."

"And where are your parents?" the man asked.

"They're probably at church right now," Joshua replied.

"Well, son, don't you think it would be better for you to go to your parents' church today?"

"But I saw this church, and I knew Jesus was here," Joshua said. "So I came to see him!"

"Well, son, I think it would be best if you were to run along home and go see Jesus in your own church in your own neighborhood," the man said. "You really can't stay here."

Realizing what the man was trying to do, Joshua got upset. "You just don't want me to see Jesus!" he yelled as he turned and ran out the big doors leading to the street.

Sobbing as he returned home, Joshua shouted, "God, it isn't fair! All I wanted to do was see Jesus, and they wouldn't let me in!"

Joshua shuffled along, staring at the sidewalk through his tears. Suddenly he heard footsteps behind him and felt a hand on his shoulder. He turned around, wiped his eyes, and stared in amazement.

It was Jesus!

The Lord smiled at Joshua, gave him a big hug, and said, "Don't be too upset, my son. They wouldn't let me in there either."

 WHERE TO TAKE IT FROM HERE...

It has been said that 11:00 to 12:00 every Sunday morning is the most segregated hour of the week. In John 17:20-21, Jesus prayed that his church would be "one," but we all know that it's anything but.

Few things have hurt the spread of the gospel more than Christians' lack of unity. The reason we have so many churches today is not that we have so many people who want to attend, but that we don't like worshiping with people who think or look different from us.

Jesus continued praying, "May they be brought to complete unity to let the world know that you sent me and have loved them even as you have loved me" (v. 23). If we can love each other, worship with each other, and serve with each other as brothers and sisters—regardless of our color or economic status—the world will find the gospel irresistible.

Wouldn't you?

116

Oliver

Chris deVinck had a brother named Oliver who was severely handicapped, blind, and bedridden. No one was sure whether Oliver was aware of the world around him, although he did eat when he was fed. Though he lived to be over 30, feeding him was like feeding an eight-month-old child. He required 24-hour care, which his mother gave him until the day he died. Chris remembers...

When I was in my early 20s, I met a girl, and I fell in love. After a few months I brought her home for dinner to meet my family. After the introductions and some small talk, my mother went to the kitchen to check the meal, and I asked the girl, "Would you like to see Oliver?" for I had, of course, told her about my brother.

"No," she answered. She did not want to see him. It was as if she slapped me in the face. In response I mumbled something polite and walked to the dining room.

Soon after, I met Roe, Rosemary—a dark-haired, dark-eyed, lovely girl. She asked me the names of my brothers and sisters. She bought me a copy of *The Little Prince*. She loved children. I thought she was wonderful. I brought her home after a few months to meet my family. The introductions. The small talk. We ate dinner; then it was time for me to feed Oliver. I walked into the kitchen, reached for the red bowl and the egg, cereal, milk, and banana and prepared Oliver's meal.

Then, I remember, I sheepishly asked Roe if she'd like to come upstairs and see Oliver.

"Sure," she said, and up the stairs we went. I sat on Oliver's bed as Roe stood and watched over my shoulder. I gave him his first spoonful, then his second.

"Can I do that?" she asked with ease, with freedom, with compassion. So I gave her the bowl, and she fed Oliver one spoonful at a time.

Which girl would you marry?

Today Roe and I have three children.

There's a lot of truth in the old saying, "A person who is nice to you, but not nice to others, is not a nice person."

That's one of the reasons that Jesus pointed to the outcasts of the world—those who were handicapped, those who were poor, those who were in prison, those who were considered "the least"—and said, in effect, "Those people are just like me. If you love me, then you will also love them." (See Matthew 25:31-46.)

Anyone can love the healthy, the successful, and the glamorous. There's little nobility or courage in that. But God calls us to a higher standard—to love the world just as he does. "Man looks at the outward appearance, but the Lord looks at the heart" (1 Samuel 16:7).

One Expensive Pearl

Lord's jewelry store had thousands of beautiful gems on display. Some were reasonably priced, others were very expensive. But one stone in the store was more prized than all of the others. It was a flawless pearl, so beautiful that it was displayed in its own specially designed case at the front of the store. People from all over the world would travel to Lord's just to gaze upon this particular pearl's amazing beauty.

Of course people wondered about the pearl's value. No price tag was visible. Most people knew they couldn't afford it anyway, so they didn't bother to ask. Occasionally, though, someone would inquire about the price.

The owner of the store would always answer, "It will cost you every-thing you own." That was a high price, indeed, and those who had hoped to add the pearl to their jewelry collections went away disappointed. The cost was simply too high.

One day a homeless man came into the store to escape the bad weather outside. He noticed the pearl in its display case and, like every-one else, was fascinated by it. He couldn't take his eyes off it. After a while, he approached the owner of the store and asked about its cost. He received the same answer as everyone else: "It will cost you everything you own."

The homeless man didn't own much, but he was still shocked by the price. He didn't leave the store. He continued gazing at the pearl. And the more he looked at it, the more he longed to have it. Finally, he took off his overcoat, placed it in the shopping cart with his other possessions, and offered all that he owned to the owner of the jewelry store.

"I'll take it," he announced.

Without the slightest hesitation, the jeweler unlocked the case and presented the magnificent pearl to its new owner.

? WHERE TO TAKE IT FROM HERE...

When Jesus said that it was easier for a camel to go through the eye of a needle than for a rich man to enter the kingdom of God, he wasn't kidding. The pearl of great price costs all that you have (Matthew 13:45-46). The more you have, the more it will cost you.

Remember the rich young ruler? He wanted that pearl very badly but turned it down because of his wealth (Matthew 19:22). That's why Jesus warns us against acquiring too much money or possessions. We might make the mistake of valuing them more than we value the kingdom of God.

Are you afraid to let go of your possessions in order to have the pearl of great price? Keep this in mind: the pearl of great price comes with everything God owns. You will be trading what you have in exchange for what God has. And he, of course, has everything. You can trust that God will not only provide you with what you need, but also bless you with much more.

THE LITTLE RIVER

This story is attributed to the late Henri Nouwen.

Once upon a time there was a little river that said, "I can become a big river." It worked hard to get big, but in the process, encountered a huge rock. "I won't let this rock stop me," the river said. And the little river pushed and pushed until it finally made its way around the rock.

Next the river encountered a mountain. "I won't let this mountain stop me," the river said. And the little river pushed and pushed until it finally carved a canyon through the mountain.

Next the river came to an enormous forest. "I won't let all these trees stop me," the river said. And the river pushed and pushed until it finally made its way through the forest.

The river, now large and powerful, finally arrived at the edge of a vast desert. "I won't let this desert stop me," the river said.

But as the river pushed and pushed its way across the desert, the hot sand began soaking up its water until only a few puddles remained.

The river was quiet.

Then the river heard a voice from above. "My child, stop pushing. It's time to surrender. Let me lift you up. Let me take over."

The river said, "Here I am."

The sun then lifted the river up and turned it into a huge cloud. And the wind carried the river across the desert and let it rain down on the hills and valleys of the faraway fields, making them fruitful and rich.

? WHERE TO TAKE IT FROM HERE...

Ambition and determination are wonderful attributes, but, apart from God, they won't get you very far. When you're young, you tend to feel invincible. You think you can accomplish almost anything on your own. Who needs God?

But what will you do when you get to the desert? There's one up ahead, you know. There will come a time when the heat will be intense, and you won't know what to do. You won't have the strength or the resources to make it through. Your desert may contain failure, rejection, disappointment, or loss. What will you do then?

When your desert comes, you may not have the opportunity to hear the voice of God saying, "It's time to surrender." But you can hear him now. He wants you to stop pushing and give your life to him today. He wants to lift you up and make you fruitful for him in ways you never imagined. Can you hear him?

Twenty Dollars Short

Just a few days before Christmas, a postal worker at the main sorting office found an unstamped, handwritten, messy envelope addressed to God. Curious, he opened it and discovered that it was from an elderly woman who was in great distress because all of her savings—$200—had been stolen. As a result, she wouldn't have anything to eat for Christmas.

The man went to his fellow postal workers and took up a collection for the woman. They all dug deep and came up with $180. Putting the money in a plain envelope, with no note or anything, the postal workers sent it by special courier to the woman that very day.

A week later, the same postal worker noticed another unstamped letter that had been addressed to God in the same handwriting. In it, he found a brief note:

Dear God,
Thank you for the $180 that you sent me for Christmas, which would have been so bleak otherwise.
P.S. It was $20 short, but that was probably those thieving workers at the post office.

 WHERE TO TAKE IT FROM HERE...

Have you ever been criticized for trying to do the right thing? Have you ever been blamed for something you didn't do? Kind of makes you want to give up, doesn't it? After all, why knock yourself out when all you get is a slap in the face?

The feeling is understandable. That's why we should be affirming to each other and encourage each other in the church. When you see someone doing the best they can, let them know that you appreciate their effort. Don't blame them or get on their case for what they weren't able to do. Don't just notice that they were $20 short.

On the other hand, if you are the one expecting to get affirmation and praise...don't hold your breath. Instead, take comfort in the fact that you are in good company. "If you suffer for doing good and you endure it, this is commendable before God. To this you were called, because Christ suffered for you, leaving you an example, that you should follow in his steps" (1 Peter 2:20-21).

You will get a lot of criticism, and it will hurt. But remember: "Let us not become weary in doing good, for at the proper time we will reap a harvest if we do not give up" (Galatians 6:9).

The Crooked Picture

Jeff liked the way he looked in his football picture. The team photographer had posed him in a traditional action stance, which made Jeff look big, tough, and mean. Jeff liked the way he looked in the picture so much that he had an enlargement made for his parents. They immediately framed the photo and hung it on the wall.

One day Jeff came home and noticed that his picture was hanging crooked. He pushed up the side that was hanging low, stood back, and decided that it was straight. It looked good.

The next day Jeff came home and noticed that his picture was crooked again. "Maybe I didn't get it straight enough yesterday," he told himself. So once again he pushed up the low side of the picture, stepped back, and decided that it was straight. And he couldn't help admiring himself in that picture.

The next day Jeff came home and noticed the picture hanging crooked again. "Hey, who keeps messing with my picture?" he wondered aloud. "I'm sure I had it straight yesterday." Once again Jeff straightened the picture and walked away, wondering if it would be crooked again tomorrow.

Sure enough, it was.

Jeff stared at the picture for a moment before an idea occurred to him. On the back of the frame was a horizontal wire that caught the wall hook. "Maybe the wire isn't centered on the hook," Jeff guessed. He slid the picture to the left about a quarter of an inch. When he let go, it hung straight.

The next day the picture was hanging perfectly straight, as it was every day after that.

And every day Jeff couldn't help admiring how good he looked in that picture.

WHERE TO TAKE IT FROM HERE...

A picture frame will only stay level if it's centered on the hook. If it's not, any attempt to correct the problem will only be temporary. Gravity will always pull it out of whack.

In the same way, unless we make Christ the center of our lives, we'll always be out of whack. In this case, though, sin—not gravity—is the problem. And there's nothing we can do ourselves to fix it. We can try again and again to straighten ourselves out, but eventually we will always end up right back where we started.

Is your life centered in Christ? Have you made him your Lord? If you have, you'll always look good in the sight of God—and his is the only opinion that really matters.

God's Donuts

An overweight man decided it was time to shed some pounds. He informed his coworkers that he was going on a diet and would no longer be bringing donuts to the office. He knew it would be hard to resist stopping at the bakery on the way to work, but he committed himself to remaining strong and resisting temptation.

His coworkers were surprised one morning to see him arrive at the office with a big box of donuts. When they reminded him of his diet, he just smiled.

"These are very special donuts," he explained. "When I left for the office this morning, I knew I was going to drive by the bakery, and I wondered if maybe the Lord might want me to have some donuts today. I wasn't sure, so I prayed, 'Lord, if you want me to stop and buy some donuts, let there be an open parking place directly in front of the bakery.' As you know, parking places in front of that bakery are hard to get!"

"So the parking place was there?" one of his coworkers asked.

"It was a miracle," the man replied. "The eighth time around the block, there it was!"

? **WHERE TO TAKE IT FROM HERE...**

We need to remember that God's will is not always our will. When we pray for God's will to be done, we shouldn't be trying to manipulate God into rubber-stamping what we have already decided to do. The Bible tells us that our hearts are wicked and "deceitful above all things" (Jeremiah 17:9). Most of the time, what we want to do is not what God wants us to do.

Jesus did not want to die on the cross, but rather than demanding his way, he prayed, "Father...not my will, but yours be done" (Luke 22:42). God always knows what's best for us. We must submit ourselves to doing what he wants, not what we want.

Love at First Sight

Henry was 73 years old when he moved into the rest home. Since the death of his wife two years earlier, Henry had been extremely lonely. He needed some company, someone to talk to.

After unpacking his belongings, Henry walked to the activities room, where many of the other residents were gathered. Everyone in the room was either talking, reading, playing cards, or watching television.

Suddenly Henry felt nervous about trying to make new friends at his age. He wasn't sure he had made the right decision.

As he stood in the doorway surveying the room, Henry was startled by a gentle tap on the shoulder. He turned to find a small woman staring up at him. Even though she must have been 85 years old, she had a kind face and was attractive. She said nothing but continued to stare at Henry.

Finally, Henry said, "Good day, madam. My name is Henry."

With a sparkle in her eye, the elderly woman said, "Henry, you look just like my fourth husband."

"I do?" Henry asked. "Tell me, how many husbands have you had?"

Smiling broadly, the woman replied, "Three."

? WHERE TO TAKE IT FROM HERE...

Needless to say, the woman made Henry's day. No matter how old you are, it still feels good to be wanted. Maybe you can give someone the gift of affirmation today. All kinds of lonely people need a tap on the shoulder and a reassuring smile.

Mark Twain once said, "I can live two weeks on one good compliment." Affirmation is a powerful act of grace that spreads God's love and leads to life. Let's build each other up and look for people around us every day who need a little encouragement and kindness (1 Thessalonians 5:11).

Holy Bucket!

For this simple illustration, bring out a bucket with four holes in the bottom of it. Have someone fill it with water. Of course, all the water will run out of the bucket (so you'll need to have another container to catch the water). After the water runs out, try it again. Then try it a third time. Your audience will probably wonder if you've lost your marbles. Why fill a bucket that won't hold water?

? WHERE TO TAKE IT FROM HERE...

Even though the bucket doesn't hold water, notice that the water is keeping the bucket clean!

Our daily devotions do the same thing. On days when you don't feel like doing them, don't feel like you're getting anything out of them, or have to rush through them, remember that devotions are still beneficial to you. Even if they run right through you like water comes out of this bucket, they still keep you clean. Just as taking a shower in the morning gets rid of bed head, your time alone with God can keep you from having a spiritual bad hair day. You'll feel fresh as a daisy and ready to take on whatever the world throws at you. So let those devotions run right through you!

That's My Child

The Koalas and Cubs were as evenly matched as any two soccer teams made up of five- and six-year-olds could be. In the first half of the game, neither team scored. The players scrambled all over the field in a clump, falling over their own feet, stumbling over the ball, kicking at it and missing. But none of them seemed to care. They were having fun.

During the second half, the coach of the Koalas pulled out most of his starters and sent in his substitutes—except for Scotty, who was the goalie and one of the team's best players.

The game took a dramatic turn. Apparently the coach of the Cubs was playing to win, because he left his best players in the game.

The Cubs took control of the contest and swarmed around Scotty, who was doing his best to guard the goal. Scotty was a good player but no match for the entire Cubs team. The little goalie gave it everything he had, recklessly throwing his body in front of incoming balls, trying to stop them. His parents cheered him on from the stands, yelling encouragement and advice. Eventually, though, the Cubs scored a goal.

A few minutes later the Cubs scored on Scotty again. This infuriated him and he became a raging maniac—shouting, running, diving. With all of the stamina he could muster, he tried covering two opposing players at once, but it was no use. The Cubs scored again.

After the third and fourth goals, Scotty's demeanor changed. He could see it was no use. He completely lost hope. Desperate futility was written all over his face. In the stands, his father's demeanor changed as well. He had been cheering on his son, but now he was feeling bad for him. He kept yelling, "That's okay, hang in there, son," but he was clearly feeling his son's pain.

After the fifth goal was scored, Scotty did what you would expect any six-year-old to do. He got so frustrated that he started crying. Huge crocodile tears rolled down both cheeks. He went to his knees, put his fists to his eyes and cried in anguish. He felt hopeless and brokenhearted.

The boy's father jumped up and ran onto the field in his business suit, tie, and dress shoes. While the game was still in progress, he picked up his son, hugged him, and cried with him.

He carried his son to the sidelines and said, "Scotty, I'm so proud of you. You were great out there. I came out here because I want everyone to know that you are my son."

"But daddy," the boy sobbed," I couldn't stop them. I tried, Daddy. I tried and tried, and they kept scoring on me."

"Scotty," his father said, "it doesn't matter how many times they scored on you. You're my son, and I'm proud of you. I want you to go back out there and keep playing. Finish the game. I know you want to quit, but you can't. Your team needs you. And you're probably going to get scored on again. But that doesn't matter, because you're my son."

 WHERE TO TAKE IT FROM HERE...

When you're getting scored on, it's easy to lose hope and want to give up. Chances are good you get scored on every day. Like Scotty, you may recklessly throw your body in every direction. You fume and rage, you struggle with temptation and sin with every ounce of energy you have—and Satan just laughs. He's left in his best players, and he's playing to win.

Perhaps you've been scored on a few times lately. You may have found yourself on your knees, crying out in anguish over your sin, your guilt, your shame. You can count on your Father in heaven to rush out onto the field. He'll pick you up, hold you in his arms, and say, "Child, I'm so proud of you. You were great out there! I want everybody to know that you're mine and that I am yours. And remember this—because I control the outcome of this game, I declare you the winner!"

Soaring

Everybody is gifted in some way. Patrick's gift was the ability to fly. He'd had the gift since he was a toddler. Patrick's mother found him sitting on top of a bookshelf or the fireplace mantle many times and assumed he had climbed up there.

When he was five, she found him on the roof of the garage and asked how he'd gotten there.

"Flew," he said.

"Children do not fly," his mother told him.

Patrick didn't know that. After that, he didn't fly anymore. A few times he dreamed of flying and woke up on the front lawn. His parents said he was sleepwalking, and his mother bought him a nice pair of pajamas in case he should do it again and the neighbors should see him.

It was when Patrick woke up on the roof of the house that his parents took him to a doctor.

"Children do not fly," the doctor said when Patrick made the mistake of telling him about the dreams. The doctor gave him some pills to make him sleep better, but Patrick quit taking them because when he did he couldn't remembered his dreams the next morning.

When he was 12 he started having the flying dreams every night. He rarely woke up in his bed, but he didn't say anything to his parents about it. He locked the window each night before he went to bed, but sometimes he still woke up outside.

When he was 14 his parents took him to a therapist. The therapist concluded that Patrick's dreams were symbolic of his need to escape from something terrible. He thought that some type of long-term abuse was causing Patrick to suppress his memories and act out his feelings in dreams.

Life at home went from bad to worse. Patrick's mother was horribly embarrassed by the whole thing, and his father simply repeated the phrase he'd used since Patrick's childhood: "Just snap out of it."

When Patrick turned 16 he was removed from his parents' custody and placed in a special facility for young people with his form of dementia. His first night in the facility he stood at his window and gazed out at

the sky. When the pretty girl he'd met in the dining hall floated past his window you could have knocked him over with a feather.

She smiled at him and waved. Soon she was joined by two more teens who briefly worked the lock on Patrick's window and opened it from the outside.

"Ready?" the pretty girl asked.

Patrick smiled and flew off with them.

 WHERE TO TAKE IT FROM HERE...

When God created you, he gave you gifts, talents, and abilities that are uniquely for you. They may not include the ability to fly, but as you grow older, you'll discover just what they are. You may have a sharp wit and see the funny side of situations. You may be inquisitive and want to investigate everything you see. You may be creative and have a desire to invent something new.

But don't be surprised if your gifts also cause problems for you. Some people believe everyone should be the same—that everyone should be normal. If you're too smart or too friendly or too responsible...well, others may feel a little threatened by that.

Find out what makes you unique. For some clues, check the Bible—after all, God's the one who created you. Romans 12:2 says, "Do not conform any longer to the pattern of this world." Don't be like everyone else. You are God's special creation, and he has big plans for your life—plans that are different from everyone else's. Some of those plans may not even be normal!

"We have different gifts, according to the grace given us...If it is serving, let him serve; if it is teaching, let him teach; if it is encouraging, let him encourage; if it is contributing to the needs of others, let him give generously; if it is leadership, let him govern diligently; if it is showing mercy, let him do it cheerfully" (Romans 12:6-8).

Find out what your gift is, and start flying!

The Giant

For 35 years the Giant sat abandoned in the work yard of the cathedral of Florence.

The Giant was a block of pure white marble, 18 feet tall and weighing several tons. However, a gaping hole that penetrated deep into the column's side made it virtually useless. Many sculptors had examined the Giant, hoping they could find a use for it, but they all eventually rejected it because they couldn't figure out a way to work around the gouge.

However, when Michelangelo spotted the Giant, he saw a magnificent rough-hewn stone from which he could carve what would become his masterpiece, David the Giant Killer. In 1501, his petition to sculpt the Giant was granted.

As Irving Stone wrote in his book *The Agony and the Ecstasy*, Michelangelo solved the problem of the gouge by "tilting his figure twenty degrees inside the column...so that David's left side could be fitted into the remaining marble. With hammer and chisel in hand, he found [himself] impatient for that first moment when a flicker of a buried image shone through, when the block became a source of life that communicated with him."

? WHERE TO TAKE IT FROM HERE...

Are you like the Giant? Do you have a flaw that you or someone else believes renders you useless? Have you felt rejected or abandoned and wondered if you'll ever do anything significant with your life?

While others may overlook you, God is the supreme artist who looks beyond your flaws and sees the image buried inside that's waiting to come out. He wants to chip away at what doesn't belong—perhaps a sin in your life, a bad habit, or a negative attitude that keeps you from being what God wants you to be. He wants to get started today.

Don't forget: that buried image inside each one of us is the image of God himself.

THE CHOICE

Centuries ago in China a teacher would call one of his students to the front of the room. He would hold out both hands and explain to the chosen student that one hand held a valuable gold coin and the other was empty. He would invite the chosen student to choose one hand or the other. If the student chose the coin, he would be allowed to keep it. But if he chose the empty hand, the teacher would strike the boy with his clenched fist. If the student decided not to choose at all, he could return to his seat.

This ritual was practiced each day in the teacher's classroom. Because the students knew of the teacher's strength and skill as a fighter, they were afraid to make a choice. They knew that to be hit by him would result in serious injury.

On the rare occasion that a student would choose a hand, the teacher would ask, "Are you sure?"

As the student looked more closely at the teacher's hard fist and even harder scowl, he would invariably change his mind and hurry back to his seat.

Finally, Chin was called to front of the room. Chin's father had died in the wars five years before and his family was having trouble getting by. Chin needed the gold coin.

The instructor held out his fists. Chin studied both hands for a long time. His classmates stared at him, expecting him to simply return to his seat as each of them had done. Finally Chin pointed to the teacher's left fist.

"Are you sure?" the instructor asked.

Chin nodded.

"Would you like to forget about your choice and return to your seat?"

Chin shook his head no.

The instructor's fist shot out and struck Chin squarely in the face, knocking him to the floor.

Chin lay on the floor looking up at his teacher in a daze. Then the instructor turned both fists over and revealed that each of them held a gold coin.

"You can not expect anything for free," the teacher told his class.

"There is a price that comes with everything."

The teacher helped Chin to his feet, smiled, and placed the gold coins into his hand. He never repeated the exercise again.

WHERE TO TAKE IT FROM HERE...

People today are afraid to make choices. Like the students in the classroom, they are afraid of failure. They are afraid of pain. They are afraid of commitment. They are afraid that it might cost them something.

Take marriage, for example. Many young people today choose not to marry because they know that commitment to one person will require a good deal of effort and self-denial. They would rather live their lives selfishly, not having to sacrifice to meet the needs of another person.

Life is full of choices like that. And contrary to popular belief, the best things in life are not free. They are always costly—but worth it.

The Bible sets before us some very clear choices: "Choose for yourselves this day whom you will serve" (Joshua 24:15). Do you have the courage to step out from the crowd and choose the way that offers the greatest reward?

Jesus said, "Enter through the narrow gate. For wide is the gate and broad is the road that leads to destruction, and many enter through it. But small is the gate and narrow the road that leads to life, and only a few find it" (Matthew 7:13-14).

ThEy Said yES

Sietske Postma had just finished her training to become an elementary school teacher when the Nazi army invaded her country of Holland. Sietske lived in a small country village with her father Djoerd, a woodworker, and her younger brother.

Though they were not politically active, the family was shocked by those in their town who viewed Nazi control as a desirable thing and even more shocked by those who enlisted in the German army or became supporters of the Nazi party.

Initially, the Germans interfered very little in the lives of the people of Holland. As the war continued, though, the Nazis instituted their cruel program of Jewish identification, deportation, and eventual extermination.

One day when the Postma family walked through the entrance to their little country town, they found a sign had been posted which read "DOGS AND JEWS FORBIDDEN."

Word quickly spread that anyone who attempted to stand in the way of the Nazis' efforts to eliminate the Jews would suffer the same fate as the Jews.

Devout Christians, Sietske and her family prayed fervently for God to intervene in the situation.

On a crisp March evening in 1943, the pastor of a local church paid the Postma family a visit. After tea and sweets were served and small talk was made, the pastor's face became serious. "I want to tell you the real reason for my stopping by tonight," he said in a sober, hushed tone.

The three faces of the Postma family stared in puzzlement.

"I was wondering if you would consider taking in someone," he said slowly.

That someone, of course, was a Jew. A person to be hidden from, not only snooping Gestapo agents, but even from the Postmas' neighbors. A person to be fed, clothed, entertained—but never revealed. A person whose mere presence in the home could result in a trip to the gas chamber or a bullet to the head.

The Postmas knew that saying yes to this request would change their family forever. They knew they would have to live with caution, subterfuge, anxiety, and even terror as the Postma house would certainly be searched more than once by Nazi soldiers.

Without hesitation Djoerd Postma said, "Yes."

"How about a Jewish girl?" the pastor asked.

Djoerd looked at his daughter, Sietske, who quickly replied, "Yes!"

After all, the Postmas never felt that it was their pastor asking them to risk their lives, but that it was the voice of God.

Because they said yes, 22-year-old Nurit Hegt lived with them until the fall of Germany in 1945. Because they said yes, Nurit, the only surviving member of her family, grew to adulthood and eventually moved to Israel, where she married and raised a family.

Because the Postmas said yes, Tree E-37 was planted in their memory on the Avenue of Righteousness in the city of Jerusalem.

 WHERE TO TAKE IT FROM HERE...

What is God calling you to do? Are you willing to say yes? It may cost you your friends. It may cost you some popularity. It may cost you things you value highly. It may cost you your life.

But when you say yes to God, you can be assured that your life will take on new meaning and purpose. And you will not be alone. When Jesus gave his disciples his great commission to go and make disciples, he told them, "Surely I am with you always" (Matthew 28:20). He did not spare them from persecution or death, but he enabled them to change the course of history. Because they said yes, we have the good news that leads to eternal life.

The Christian life is more than willingness to do what Jesus asks us to do—it is costly obedience. "If anyone would come after me, let him deny himself and take up his cross and follow me" (Matthew 16:24). Can you say yes to that?

Stepping

Kyle walked beside his best friend Rico. They followed a girl named Rachel whom Kyle had wanted to get to know all school year. He had been watching her during lunch in the cafeteria. A few times she caught him staring and smiled back, but she had never spoken to him until today.

"A bunch of us are going stepping later," she said. "Do you want to come?"

"Sure," Kyle said. He immediately wished he'd kept his mouth shut. Stepping. What was he thinking? Kids get killed going stepping. The counselors and teachers had all talked about how dangerous it was. There were posters all over the library: "Stepping kills" and "This is your brain after you've gone stepping."

He'd promised his mother he would never ever go stepping. But he'd just accepted an invitation from the prettiest girl in school.

He asked Rico to come along for moral support. Rico would try anything once. Plus, Rico was a tall, geeky guy who really wanted to fit in with the cool crowd and would probably see this as his chance. If Kyle got scared, Rico would push him forward. If he got hurt, Rico would be there to help.

As it turned out, "a bunch of us" meant two other teens from Kyle's class. So there were five of them all together.

"Aw, man, what are they doing here?" It was Greg Irons, a jerk from Kyle's health class. He gave Kyle and Rico a disgusted look.

"I invited Kyle," Rachel said. It seemed as though she was in charge of the group, because Greg shut up after that. The other stepper was a girl named Heather. Kyle had seen her in band but had never spoken to her. She was popular.

"We can't do this." Kyle whispered to Rico.

"Yes, we can," Rico said. "We can't back out now. I'm not going to be a geek the rest of my life."

The group stood silently for a moment looking at each other. "Okay, let's do this," Rachel said "Who's first?"

"I am," Greg said. He said it looking at Kyle, as if he were challenging him by volunteering to go first.

"Okay," Rachel said.

Greg smirked at Kyle. "He won't do it. He's gonna back out. Look at him."

"You said you were gonna go, so go," Kyle replied.

Greg walked backward from the group about ten feet before turning to face away from them. Without another word, he went stepping.

"Cool," Rachel said. "Heather?"

Heather looked nervous. "You go. I'll wait."

"Scared?" Rachel asked. Her voice had taken on a mean tone that Kyle didn't like. He wasn't sure he wanted to spend time with this girl anymore.

"No," Heather said. She turned away and walked to where Greg had "stepped" and, without looking back, followed him.

"I'm next," Rachel said. She looked at Kyle. "You're going to come after me, aren't you?"

"Sure," Kyle said. He did it again. He couldn't believe it. For the second time, he had blindly agreed to do something completely stupid and dangerous.

Rachel went stepping with a flourish that suited her looks.

"We gotta do it now," Rico said.

"We don't have to do it now," Kyle said. "They'll never know we didn't go, too."

"Sure they will," Rico said with anger in his voice. "Look, you can stay. But I'm going." Rico walked away from his best friend and followed the crowd.

Kyle stood there looking at the spot where the others had gone. Mom's gonna kill me, he thought and walked forward.

He could already hear the sirens as he stood on the edge of the apartment building. Crowds were gathering far below.

"This is really stupid," Kyle said. Then he went stepping, too.

(?) WHERE TO TAKE IT FROM HERE...

No one has to tell you that doing drugs or alcohol is stupid. You know that already. You've seen what it's done to the lives of people all around you. You've seen the posters and heard the lectures. It sounds cool and may even provide a thrill—sort of like jumping off a tall building—but down

deep you know how stupid it is.

Why do so many kids feel a need to do it anyway?

In most cases, it's all about acceptance. The desire to fit in with the crowd. The need to be liked by others and perceived as cool.

Satan tempted Jesus by taking him to the top of the tallest building in Jerusalem (Matthew 4:5). He thought he could tempt Jesus with some pretty cool stepping. He said, "Throw yourself down from this high place, and let's see if you survive. Let's see if God's angels really show up to rescue you!" That would have been seriously cool. Everyone who saw it would have been very impressed, and Jesus would have become famous—a celebrity for sure!

But Jesus was smart enough to know that it didn't matter what people thought of him. The only audience that really mattered to Jesus was his Father in heaven. When Jesus was baptized, the voice of God said, "This is my Son, whom I love; with him I am well pleased" (Matthew 3:17). So Jesus told the devil to get lost.

Next time your friends ask you to go stepping, tell them to get lost, too.

140 ———————————————

The Parable of the Baseball Team

Behold, a team went forth to play a game of baseball.

Just as the umpire was saying, "Batter up," the catcher for the home team arrived and took his place behind the plate. The center fielder didn't show up at all but sent his regrets. The third baseman likewise failed to come to the game, having been up late the night before. The shortstop was present, but left his glove at home. Two of the substitute fielders were away on a weekend trip but said they were there in spirit.

The pitcher went to the mound and looked around for his teammates. But his heart was heavy, for their positions were empty. The game was announced, the visitors were in the stands, and there was nothing to do but pitch the ball and hope for the best. But in addition to pitching, he had to cover first and third base, as well as short and center field.

When the absent players heard that their team had lost, they were very upset. They held a meeting and decided to get a new pitcher.

(?) WHERE TO TAKE IT FROM HERE...

When things aren't going well in the church or the youth group, our tendency is to blame the leadership. The pastor, the youth minister, or other leaders are easy targets because they are most visible.

But like a baseball team, the church can't survive without everyone pulling their weight. The pitcher—the pastor—is important, but unless everyone else shows up and fields their position or gets a hit, the game will be lost.

The Bible never makes a distinction between professional ministers (clergy) and "ordinary Christians" (laity). Instead, everyone is a minister, each having different gifts and abilities (see 1 Corinthians 12, Romans 12, and Ephesians 4). A baseball team can't win with players who don't play. Nor can a church with ministers who don't minister.

Saving Private Ryan

One of the most powerful films in recent history is Steven Spielberg's *Saving Private Ryan*. The film begins on D-Day, June 6, 1944, as the Nazis were advancing across Western Europe. Faced with the ugly possibility of defeat, the Allied powers staged on the beaches of Normandy the greatest military invasion in history. Their goal was to cripple the German army and ultimately force Hitler and his army into retreat.

Following the bloody battle, Captain John Miller (played by Tom Hanks) and his surviving company of soldiers receive very unusual orders from their commander. They must locate and rescue a solder, Private James Ryan (played by Matt Damon), who is fighting somewhere behind enemy lines. We are told that Ryan and his three older brothers enlisted in the Army. What Private Ryan doesn't know is that all three of his brothers perished during the Normandy invasion. To spare Private Ryan's mother the anguish of losing all four of her sons, Miller and his men must find James and bring him back alive.

As Miller and his eight men move deeper into enemy territory in search of Ryan, they engage in an intense debate about why one man's life is so important that they should risk theirs. "This Ryan better be worth it," Miller says. "He better go home and cure some disease or invent a new longer-lasting light bulb."

Despite their misgivings, Captain Miller's band of soldiers bravely carry out their orders, with several of them paying the ultimate price as they successfully locate and rescue the young soldier. In the final battle scene, Miller takes a bullet that will ultimately cost him his life. But before he dies, he whispers to Private Ryan, who is kneeling by his side, "Earn this...earn it."

The movie ends with a scene set some fifty years after the war, with the elderly James Ryan standing over Captain Miller's grave at Arlington National Cemetery. With a trembling voice, he says, "Every day I think about what you said to me that day on the bridge. I've tried to live my life the best I could. I hope that was enough...I hope I earned what you did for me."

In the movie, Ryan then asks his wife, "Have I been a good man?" For 50 years, he was tormented by the realization that he could never do enough to earn what Captain Miller and his men did for him.

Contrast that with Jesus, who gave his life so that we could live. His dying words were not "Earn this." Instead, he said, "It is finished!"

Had Jesus said, "Earn this," you would have quickly come to realize that there's no way to earn what it cost for Jesus to give his life for yours. To spend a lifetime trying to earn your salvation only leads to frustration and despair.

That's why Jesus said, "It is finished!" He declared once and for all that nothing more needs to be done. You don't have to earn it. The free gift of salvation is yours—no strings attached. Just believe and accept him as your savior and friend.

Does that mean we live our lives as if nothing happened? Do we go on living as we did before? "By no means!" writes Paul in Romans 6:2. Instead, we demonstrate that we have new life in Christ by living in obedience to him. Our good works won't earn our salvation, but they will provide evidence that we have gratefully received it.

Ramu

In 1954, a small boy was found outside a hospital in Balrampur, India. Doctors were perplexed by his condition and, after many examinations, were unsure of how to treat him.

The boy had calloused knees and hands, as if he had spent most of his young life on all fours. He had hideously pointed teeth with cracks in his gums, suggesting that he had bitten into stone or very hard wood. He had scars on the back of his neck, suggesting that he had been dragged around by animals with sharp teeth. He spoke no discernible language and seemed unable to communicate with anyone. He had no name, so the hospital staff called him "Ramu."

Ramu showed no interest in other children and was especially frightened by adults. But one day, a hospital employee took Ramu and some other children for a visit to the zoo. The employee noticed that Ramu became extremely excited when he saw the wolf pen. Ramu called to the wolves and seemed to be able to communicate with them.

This led doctors to conduct an experiment. They found that Ramu lapped milk out of a glass rather than drinking it. He tore apart his food and chewed on meat bones for hours at a time. The doctors finally concluded that Ramu was a *ghadya ka bacha*, or wolf boy, who had grown up with the wild animals and, therefore, behaved more like a wolf than a human being.

 WHERE TO TAKE IT FROM HERE...

Ramu wasn't actually a wolf boy, of course. He was a human being—a little boy like all little boys—"fearfully and wonderfully made" (Psalm 139:14) in the image of his heavenly Father. But he grew up with wolves and became just like one of them.

You may not have to worry about developing wolflike tendencies, but if you allow yourself to be surrounded by people who don't share your beliefs and priorities, you run the risk of becoming just like them. First Corinthians 15:33 reminds us, "Bad company corrupts good character."

Catch-22

The next time you fly on a commercial airline, check out the safety instruction card that is usually found in the seat pocket in front of you. Here's what one United Airlines card said:

> If you are sitting in an exit row and you cannot understand this card or cannot see well enough to follow these instructions, please tell a crew member.

Obviously, those directions present a slight problem. If people can't understand the card or see the instructions, how can they be expected to tell a crewmember about it? Sounds like a Catch-22.

 **WHERE TO TAKE IT FROM HERE...**

Believe it or not, the Bible is a lot like that safety instruction card. Many people read Scripture without understanding it. It makes absolutely no sense to them—not because they lack eyesight or reading ability, but because they lack faith. As Paul wrote, "For the message of the cross is foolishness to those who are perishing, but to us who are being saved it is the power of God" (1 Corinthians 1:18).

In other words, unless you have faith, you won't understand the Bible. But unless you understand the Bible, you won't have faith. Sounds like another Catch-22.

That's why we have the Holy Spirit. When we come to the Bible with a willingness to learn, God sends his Holy Spirit to reveal what it is saying— even "the deep things of God" (1 Corinthians 2:10). Whenever you study God's Word with an open heart, the Holy Spirit helps you understand it and grow stronger in your faith.

God also uses people like us to explain the Bible to unbelievers. When someone tells you they don't understand the Bible, that's like an airline passenger telling a flight attendant they don't understand the safety instruction card. It's up to us to make it clear.

PROVERBS TO LIVE BY

a first-grade teacher gave her students the first half of a proverb and asked them to come up with the rest. Here are just a few of the responses she received:

Better to be safe than...punch a fifth grader.
Strike while the...bug is close.
It's always darkest before...daylight savings time.
Never underestimate the power of...termites.
You can lead a horse to water but...how?
Don't bite the hand that...looks dirty.
No news is...impossible.
A miss is as good as a...mister.
You can't teach an old dog...arithmetic.
If you lie down with dogs, you...stink in the morning.
The pen is mightier than...the pigs.
An idle mind is...a good way to go to sleep.
Where there's smoke, there's...lung cancer.
A penny saved is...not very much.
Two's company, three's...the Musketeers.
Children should be seen and not...spanked.
If at first you don't succeed...get new batteries.
You get out of something what you...see pictured on the box.
When the blind lead the blind...get out of the way.
There is no fool like...Uncle George.
Laugh and the whole world laughs with you, cry and....you have to blow your nose.

 WHERE TO TAKE IT FROM HERE...

Many people today are like those first graders when it comes to the truth of Scripture. For example, Jesus said, "No one comes to the Father except through me" (John 14:6). But how many people think that verse says, "No one comes to the Father except through attending the right church...or

staying away from drugs and alcohol...or giving money to the poor"?

Jesus said, "If anyone would come after me, he must deny himself, take up his cross and follow me" (Matthew 16:24). But how many people believe this version: "If anyone would come after me, let him deny himself nothing, because God wants us to grow rich!"

You can't rewrite the truth of the gospel to suit yourself. That's why it's so important to study God's Word and memorize it. Only then will you know the truth that can set you free.

WINNERS

Below are two quizzes. See how well you do on each one.

Quiz 1
1. Name the MVPs of the last World Series, Super Bowl, Stanley Cup finals, and NBA finals.
2. Name the winner of the last Heisman Trophy.
3. Name the winner of the last Miss America contest.
4. Name five Nobel or Pulitzer prize winners.
5. Name five winners of last year's Academy Awards.
6. Name the winner of the largest state lottery in history.
7. Name the winner of the last Indianapolis 500 or Kentucky Derby.
8. Name five winners of last year's Grammy Awards.

Quiz 2
1. Name a teacher who has helped you learn and grow as a person.
2. Name five friends who have been there for you during good times and bad.
3. Name three adults who have been excellent role models for you.
4. Name two people who love you and pray for you regularly.
5. Name someone who makes you laugh.
6. Name someone who has given you something of great value.
7. Name a hero whose life story has inspired you.
8. Name someone has helped you through a difficult time.

? WHERE TO TAKE IT FROM HERE...

If you're like most people, you probably flunked the first quiz. Few of us remember the big names and headline grabbers of yesterday. Yet these people are not second-rate achievers. They're the best in their fields. You'd think they'd be easy to remember.

However, when the lights go off, the applause dies down, and the trophies begin to tarnish, their achievements are often forgotten. The accolades and awards eventually fade into oblivion with their owners.

How did you do on the second quiz? It was probably much easier for you, wasn't it? That's because the people we remember most in our lives are not necessarily those who have the most money or the most awards or the most fame. Usually they are the people who care about us, who know us, or who have made a significant contribution to our lives.

Don't just seek after fame and fortune. If you want to be remembered—if you want to leave a legacy—be a person who cares about others. Keep in mind that the most revered person in history came not to get fame or fortune for himself, but "made himself nothing...humbled himself and became obedient to death—even death on a cross" (Philippians 2:7-8).

First Class

On a British Airways flight from Johannesburg, South Africa, a wealthy middle-aged white woman found herself sitting next to a black gentleman. She called the cabin crew attendant over to complain about her seating.

"What seems to be the problem, madam?" asked the attendant.

"Can't you see?" the woman snapped loudly, "You've seated me next to a kaffir. I can't possibly sit next to this disgusting man. Find me another seat!"

"Please calm down, madam," the attendant replied. "I believe the economy section is full today, but I'll check to see if we have any upgraded seats available in club or first class."

The woman struck a snooty pose, looking condescendingly at the embarrassed black man beside her (not to mention many of the outraged passengers).

A few minutes later the cabin attendant returned with good news. "Madam, as I suspected, our economy section is full. I've spoken to the cabin services director, and business class is also full. However, we do have one seat available in first class."

The woman gave the people around her a smug grin.

The flight attendant continued, "Please realize, it is most extraordinary to make this kind of upgrade, and I have had to get special permission from the captain. But, given the extreme circumstances, the captain felt it was outrageous that someone should be forced to sit next to such a disgusting person."

With that, she turned to the black man and said, "Sir, if you'd like to get your things, I have your first-class seat ready for you."

As the man got up and walked to the front of the plane, the surrounding passengers gave him a standing ovation.

WHERE TO TAKE IT FROM HERE...

"Do not judge, or you too will be judged. For in the same way you judge others, you will be judged, and with the measure you use, it will be measured to you" (Matthew 7:1-2).

The Dirty Dollar

Take a $20 bill (or any bill) and hold it up in front of the group. Ask who would like to have it. Obviously, everyone will probably raise a hand.

Crumple up the bill, throw it on the floor, and step on it. Then pick it up and ask, "Now, who would like this money?" Once again, you should expect an affirmative response from everyone.

Next, spit on the bill, rub dirt on it, dunk it in a toilet, or otherwise abuse it. Then ask who would be willing to take it. Chances are pretty good that everyone will still be willing to take the money off your hands.

 WHERE TO TAKE IT FROM HERE...

God knows our true value and loves us not because we look good or do all the right things, but because we have inherent worth as his children. In the same way, we shouldn't judge people by what's on the outside, but by what's on the inside. Everyone is a child of God and worthy of respect. You can take this illustration another step, either to emphasize evangelism or to encourage Christian young people to "walk the talk."

After trashing the original $20 bill and making it look as bad as you can, take another brand-new $20 bill and hold it up for comparison.

Obviously, both of these twenties are worth the same amount of money. But if you had your choice, wouldn't you rather have the new one? If you were a $20 bill, wouldn't you rather be the new one?

God loves us even when we're a mess, but he wants us to come to Jesus Christ and be made new. You may think you can live any way you want, that it doesn't matter to God how you live. But it does! God wants you to get cleaned up, and he's provided a way for that to happen. You can't do it yourself, of course. You need Christ, who will do it for you. He'll change your life. "Therefore if anyone is in Christ, he is a new creation...The old has gone, the new has come!" (2 Corinthians 5:17)

The Man on the Hill

n old man lived on a hill that overlooked the ocean. At the bottom of the hill was a public campground where people would come to pitch their tents, hike along the beach, and play in the surf. One day the old man was looking out at the ocean from his window when he noticed a huge tidal wave bearing down on the campground. He knew that the people who occupied the campground below were doomed. He had no phone or any other way to warn them from his hillside perch. And he knew that if he attempted to run down to the campground, by the time he got there, he would be wiped out, too.

There was only one thing to do. He grabbed a book of matches and set his house on fire. Within minutes the people in the campground noticed the smoke from the fire and rushed up the hill to try to save the man. Just as the campers made it to the top, the tidal wave reached land and completely destroyed the campground and everything in it. But the people were saved.

? WHERE TO TAKE IT FROM HERE...

The man on the hill sacrificed his home to save the lives of people he didn't even know. There was no other way. God did much more than that when he sacrificed his son on our behalf. There was no other way.

Just as the fire on the hill drew people away from the death and destruction of the tidal wave, so the cross draws people away from their lives of sin.

Jesus said, "But I, when I am lifted up from the earth, will draw all men to myself" (John 12:32). When we run to the cross, we escape the death and destruction of sin. It's the only way to salvation.

Giving It Up for a Friend

Kay Poe and Esther Kim grew up as best friends and fierce competitors. Their sport was tae kwon do, a form of martial arts that was featured for the first time in the 2000 Sydney Olympics. As Kay and Esther got older, they found themselves in different weight classes, so they rarely met in competition. In the pre-Olympic trials they were each favored to win their classes.

There was just one problem. The United States would be sending representatives from only two of the four weight classes to the Olympics, so only one of them would be able to go to Sydney.

In the final moments of the final bout in her weight class Kay seriously dislocated her kneecap. In spite of her injury, she fought strongly enough to win the match and her division. As she hobbled off the floor her Olympic dreams seemed over. She still had one more match to win—this one against her friend Esther Kim.

Esther saw her coach carrying her friend Kay back to the dressing room. The outcome of the final match was a no-brainer. All Esther had to do was show up, and she was on her way to the Olympics. Her injured friend didn't have a chance. Esther knew that she, not Kay, would be going to the Olympics.

But in a moment of incredible love and sacrifice, Esther made a decision to bow out of the final match and concede victory to her injured friend. She gave up her Olympic dream so that Kay could realize hers.

When Esther informed Kay of her decision, Kay protested.

"Don't you dare argue with me about this," Esther told her. They held each other and cried. "Please don't think I'm throwing my dreams away," Esther said, "because I'm not. I'm putting my dreams in you."

Esther signed the scorecard, withdrawing from the match. Then the two friends had to bow to each other on the mat to make it official. Kay's coach helped her walk to one side of the mat. Esther walked to the other. By the time they reached the referee in the middle, tears flowed freely. The two young women bowed. The referee signaled Poe the winner. Then the women locked arms, sobbing. As they slowly walked off the mat together, the tae kwon do officials stood and bowed while fans applauded them both.

Esther later told stunned reporters, "There's more than one way to be a champion."

 **WHERE TO TAKE IT FROM HERE...**

Esther Kim may not have competed in the Olympic Games, but she is a champion nonetheless. Not only is she a champion in her chosen sport, she's a champion in love. Jesus said, "Greater love has no one than this, that one lay down his life for his friends" (John 15:13). Esther laid down her life's dream so that her friend could have hers. That makes her a champion indeed.

No Secrets

As their wedding day approached, a young couple grew apprehensive. Each had a problem they had never before shared with anyone, not even each other.

The groom-to-be decided to ask his father for advice. "Father," he said, "I'm concerned about the success of my marriage. I love my fiancée very much, but I have smelly feet. I'm afraid that my future wife will find them, and me, disgusting."

"No problem," said his father, "All you have to do is wash your feet as often as possible and always wear socks, even to bed."

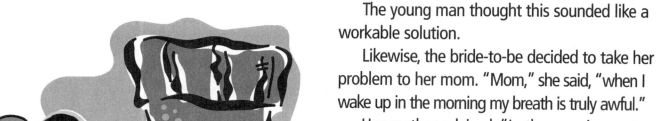

The young man thought this sounded like a workable solution.

Likewise, the bride-to-be decided to take her problem to her mom. "Mom," she said, "when I wake up in the morning my breath is truly awful."

Her mother advised, "In the morning, get straight out of bed, head for the bathroom, and brush your teeth. Don't say a word until you've brushed them—not a word."

The bride-to-be thought the suggestion was certainly worth a try.

The loving couple was finally married in a beautiful ceremony. Not forgetting the advice each had received—he with his perpetual socks and she with her morning silence—they managed quite well.

About six months later, shortly before dawn, the husband woke up horrified to discover that one of his socks had come off during the night. Fearful of the consequences, he frantically started searching the bed. This, of course, woke his bride. Without thinking, she blurted out, "What on earth are you doing?"

"Oh no!" he gasped as he recoiled in shock. "You've swallowed my sock!"

Maybe you don't have stinky feet or sewer breath, but chances are you have some embarrassing or disgusting secrets that you hope nobody ever finds out about.

Everybody has a few secrets they prefer to keep from parents and friends, and even from husbands and wives. At a conference where he was speaking, Tony Campolo once said, "If I knew everything about you people, I probably wouldn't have accepted your invitation to speak. But if you knew everything about me, you probably wouldn't have invited me to come."

There's nothing wrong with protecting your privacy. It's okay to have secrets. Some things you should just keep to yourself.

But you can't hide anything from God. He knows you very well. Do you know how many hairs are on your head? God does.

In spite of all that he knows, God still loves you. In fact, he wants to know more about you because he's interested in you and cares about you.

He thinks the world of you. He loves you so much that he gave his only son to die for you. And all he asks in return is your acceptance of that love.

Don't try to hide who you are or what you've done from God. Don't think that just because you have some dirty laundry in your past God will automatically reject you. He won't. There is nothing you can do that will separate you from the love of God (Romans 8:39). God loves you—bad breath, smelly feet, and all.

An Altitude Problem

A few years ago, a couple of adventurers tried to become the first to circle the globe in a hot air balloon. They took off from St. Louis, Missouri, rose to 24,000 feet, and started eastward across the Atlantic Ocean toward Africa.

The prevailing winds carried the balloonists on a direct course for Libya, which was a big problem. Libya is ruled by a dictator who hates Americans and doesn't want American balloons flying over his country. There was a pretty good chance that the balloon would be shot down if it crossed Libyan air space.

This brings up another big problem. Hot air balloons aren't easy to turn. In fact, they can't be turned at all. They're at the mercy of the wind.

But they can find different winds. This is done by changing altitude. At a higher or lower altitude, a balloonist can usually find a crosswind blowing in a different direction.

So the quick thinking adventurers started letting hot air out of their balloon and dropped 6,000 feet. At that altitude, they found a wind that was blowing south rather than east. Once they were safely to the south of Libya and its missiles, they heated up the balloon, rose almost 10,000 feet, and caught another wind that was blowing eastward toward their destination.

 WHERE TO TAKE IT FROM HERE...

Balloonists are at the mercy of the wind and can go only in the direction that the wind is blowing. Likewise, some people think they are at the mercy of circumstances. "Stuff happens," they say, "and there's nothing you can do about it."

But there is something you can do.

Just as balloonists can change their altitude, so you can change your attitude. And when you change your attitude, you change your direction. You're no longer at the mercy of circumstances.

Remember what Paul wrote when he was in prison: "Rejoice in the Lord always. I will say it again: Rejoice!" (Philippians 4:4.) Paul wasn't a prisoner to his circumstances. In his heart, he was free. By changing his attitude, he was able to change the world.

DOOMED

An explorer deep in the Amazon jungle found himself surrounded by a group of bloodthirsty cannibals. The explorer said quietly to himself, "I'm doomed!"

Suddenly a ray of light appeared from the sky, and a voice boomed out, "No, my son, you are not doomed. Pick up that stone at your feet and bash in the head of the chief standing in front of you."

The explorer picked up the stone and attacked the chief. After a few swift blows, he looked down at the chief's lifeless body. The rest of the cannibals stared silently at the explorer.

Then the voice boomed out again: "Okay...now you're doomed."

? WHERE TO TAKE IT FROM HERE...

Sometimes it's a good idea to double-check your sources. Not every voice that sounds authoritative is actually looking out for your best interests. You can find advice just about anywhere these days, and much of it can sound pretty convincing. But how do you know what to believe or who to trust?

When you're trying to decide what to do in a tough situation, how do you determine what God's will is? You may not hear the voice of God booming from the heavens, but what about that "still, small voice" that prompts you in a particular direction. How do you know whether or not that voice can be trusted?

You must always test what you hear against the Bible. If someone or something is prompting you to do something that contradicts the Word of God, then it can't possibly be from God. Some people commit sin and say, "God led me to do it." But they're mistaken. It's impossible for God to commit sin or to recommend it (1 John 3:8-9).

If you want to be prepared for the difficult situations you may face, don't wait for God to give you directions in a booming voice from heaven. Study his Word. You'll be ready for just about anything that comes along. (see 2 Timothy 2:15).

The First Shall Be Last

You've heard of the Tour de France, the famous bicycle race in Europe. But you've probably never heard of the world's shortest bicycle race in India.

All of the racers line up at the starting line, ready to go. They've got their riding pants, helmets, water bottles, numbers on their backs, corporate sponsors—the whole bit.

The starting pistol goes off and the racers jump onto their bikes. But nobody goes anywhere. They all stay put. You see, the object of this race is to see who can go the shortest distance possible within the specified time limit. Racers are disqualified if their bike tips over or if their feet touch the ground. The cyclists inch forward just enough to keep their bikes balanced. They can't go backward.

At the end of the race, when the gun goes off, the cyclists who have gone the farthest are the losers. The racer closest to the starting line—which, in this case, is also the finish line—is the winner.

 WHERE TO TAKE IT FROM HERE...

Imagine qualifying for the Indian bicycle race without understanding the rules. When the starting gun goes off, you hop onto your bike and pedal as hard and as fast as you possibly can. You may wonder why all of the other racers are frozen like statues behind you. Maybe you chalk it up to intimidation. They're all scared of you. As your competition disappears from sight, you start thinking about how you're going to spend the prize money.

Not so fast, spandex-pants.

When this race ends, you'll be the big loser. Not because you didn't try hard to win. Not because you didn't train properly. Not because you weren't in shape. You'll lose this race because you didn't understand the rules.

Jesus has given us the rules for the race of life. And it isn't what we do. It's what God does. Jesus died on the cross to pay the penalty for our sins. Salvation is a gift. All we do is accept the gift God's given us. "For it is by grace you have been saved, through faith—and this not from yourselves, it is the gift of God—not by works, so that no one can boast" (Ephesians 2:8-9).

No Basket!

Many people who were there called it the best basketball game they'd ever seen: Westwood High versus Valley Center, to determine who would advance to the state basketball championship.

From the opening whistle the contest was a nail-biter. Players from both schools turned in the game of their lives—running, dribbling, passing, rebounding, shooting, and playing defense with an intensity that their fans had never seen before.

The momentum of the game seesawed back and forth, with the lead changing hands more than a dozen times.

With only ten seconds to go, Westwood scored a basket that put them ahead by a single point. Valley Center called time-out. The team huddled with their coach, who drew up what would most certainly be the final play. The plan was to work the clock down to two seconds, set a few screens to get their best shooter a good look at the basket, and let him try to win the game with a last-second shot.

When the whistle blew, the crowd rose to its feet. Their cheers were deafening. Westwood positioned its defense, and Valley Center brought the ball up.

As the clock ticked down to its final seconds, the Westwood fans chanted along, "FIVE...FOUR...THREE...TWO..."

The Valley Center players executed the play exactly as the coach had drawn it up. With only two seconds remaining, Valley Center's star player took his shot. The ball bounced off the rim and ricocheted off the backboard—right to a Valley Center player, who tipped it in!

The Valley Center fans went wild. Their team was going to the state finals! Or so they thought.

While the players and fans celebrated, the referees ran to the official scorer's table to make sure that the time on the clock had not expired when the ball was tipped in. With all of the noise, the referees had been unable to hear the buzzer to determine whether or not the shot was good.

The official scorer, an older man who had held the position for many years, suddenly had the game in his hands. He hesitated for a moment, but finally leaned over the table and said, "Tell the Valley Center coach I'm very sorry, but the shot was no good. Time on the clock had expired ."

That news changed everything for both teams. The Westwood players and fans started celebrating their victory while those from Valley Center were left to deal with the agony of defeat. The stunned Valley Center coach sat down on the bench with his head in his hands.

The official scorer left his table, walked over, and sat down on the bench beside him. With a tear in his eye, the older man embraced the distraught young coach on the bench and said, "Son...I'm so proud of you."

 WHERE TO TAKE IT FROM HERE...

This story, which is based on actual events, is a powerful example of the cost of living with integrity. It would have been very easy for the official scorer to give the game to his son's team. Instead, though, he chose to preserve his integrity. He did the right thing.

This story is also a powerful illustration of what God did when he allowed Jesus to die on the cross. God could have thrown the game, but he took the loss of his precious Son in order to preserve his integrity and to provide salvation for the whole world. He did the right thing.

Shake It Off

Once upon a time a farmer's mule fell into a dry well. When the farmer heard the mule's braying and realized what had happened, he determined that neither the mule nor the well was worth the trouble of saving.

Instead, he called his neighbors together and enlisted their help in burying the old mule in the well and putting him out of his misery.

Initially, the old mule was very upset. You would be, too, if you were in a deep hole and people started throwing dirt in on top of you! But as the dirt rained down on his back, the old mule had a thought. He decided that every time a shovel of dirt landed on his back, he would shake it off and step up. And that's what he did.

As the dirt cascaded down the well, the old mule kept shaking it off and stepping up.

Hours later, the exhausted mule finally stepped over the wall of the well. What was meant to bury him actually helped him!

? WHERE TO TAKE IT FROM HERE...

The next time you find yourself trapped in a seemingly hopeless situation, you know what to do: shake it off and step up! (See James 1:2.)

Unbreakable

A collector of rare antiques walked into a curio shop and noticed a beautiful piece of glass art displayed under a sign marked "Unbreakable."

"Pardon me," the man said to the storekeeper, "but what is the price of this piece?"

"One hundred thousand dollars," replied the storekeeper.

With a gasp, the man asked why the price was so high.

"Like the sign says, it's unbreakable!" the storekeeper explained.

The man examined the piece carefully and asked, "Are you certain that this piece is unbreakable?"

The storekeeper assured him that it was.

The man greatly admired the piece, so he paid the full price and took it home. There he put it on display in a protective case. He told everyone who came to admire it that it was very special—an unbreakable piece of glass.

Several weeks later, the man visited the curio shop again and explained to the storekeeper how much care he'd taken to protect and preserve the beautiful piece he'd purchased.

While looking around, the man noticed another piece of glass art beneath the unbreakable sign. It occurred to the man that he'd seen the same piece marked $500 the last time he was in the shop. He asked the storekeeper, "How can that piece be unbreakable, too? Last month when I was here, it was in the display cabinet with those other pieces, and it was marked $500!"

"No, the price is $100,000," the storekeeper replied. "It's unbreakable, now, too."

"How can you be so sure?" the man demanded.

"Because the schmuck who pays a hundred grand for this thing is going to take as much care of it as you have with yours!"

? WHERE TO TAKE IT FROM HERE...

When you know something is extremely valuable, you tend to take very good care of it. The Bible tells us that we were "bought with a price" (1 Corinthians 6:20). God paid a very high price for each of us. He sacrificed his only son so we could have eternal life. For that reason, every person you meet is of great value, because he or she is of great value to God.

How do you treat the people you encounter every day? How do you treat the members of your own family? How do you treat people who are different from you or people who have less than you do?

THE CAMEL QUESTION

baby camel asked his mother, "Mom, why do I have these huge three-toed feet?"

His mother replied, "Well, son, your toes help you stay on top of the soft sand when we trek across the desert."

A few minutes later the baby camel asked, "Mom, why do I have these long eyelashes?"

His mother replied, "Well, son, your eyelashes help keep the sand out of your eyes on our trips through the desert."

A few minutes later the baby camel asked, "Mom, why do I have these great big humps on my back?"

His mother, who was getting a little impatient with her son, replied, "Well, son, your humps store water for our long treks across the desert, so you can go without drinking for long periods of time."

"That's great, Mom," the baby camel said. "We have huge feet to stop us from sinking, long eyelashes to keep sand out of our eyes, and humps to store water. But...Mom?"

"Yes, son?"

"Why are we in the zoo?"

? WHERE TO TAKE IT FROM HERE...

God created you for a purpose. He's provided you with gifts and talents so that you can serve him and make a difference in the world.

Are you doing what God created you to do? Maybe you feel a little like the camel in the zoo. Life is easy, things are going along pretty smoothly, but you have a nagging feeling inside that maybe you aren't living up to your God-given potential.

Living in a zoo isn't all bad, but it's certainly not what camels were created to do. Living outside the will of God may not be all bad, either, but it's not what you were created to do. Let Jesus set you free and give you the abundant life that you were meant to live (John 10:10)!

The Happiest Man on Earth

Once upon a time, there was a king who had more money than he knew what to do with. He owned land as far as the eye could see. He built dozens of castles and filled them with silver and gold. He had hundreds of servants at his beck and call.

But no matter how much the king acquired, he never seemed to have enough. As a result he was a miserable man.

One day the king called for one of his servants and gave him these instructions: "I want you to scour the land from one horizon to the other and find the happiest man on earth. Once you've found him, I want you to take all that he owns and bring it to me. Kill him, if necessary. I must have what he has, because then I will be happy myself! By the way, if you fail in your mission, you will be beheaded."

After many months of searching, the servant returned. The king noticed the servant's hands were empty and became very angry. He gave the servant one minute to explain why he had disobeyed the king's orders.

With tears in his eyes, the servant looked at the king and said with a trembling voice, "Master, I did as you said. I searched from horizon to horizon looking for the happiest man on earth, and I finally found him."

The king stood and shouted at the servant, "Then why didn't you bring me this man's possessions?"

The servant replied, "Master, the happiest man on earth didn't have any."

It's no secret that rich people are often unhappy. There is no relationship between an increase in one's bank account and an increase in one's personal happiness. In fact studies show that the majority of state lottery winners say they regret having won at all. Their sudden wealth actually creates more problems for them than happiness.

Jesus said, "Blessed [or "happy"] are you who are poor" (Luke 6:20). And he wasn't just trying to make poor people feel better about themselves! The Bible tells us that Jesus himself had "no place to lay his head" (Matthew 8:20). What's more, he had no possessions of his own.

God may bless you with more than you need to get by in today's world, and if he does, you can be very grateful. But never mistake possessions for the abundant life that Jesus offers (John 10:10).

Possessions can't possibly provide you with happiness or anything else of true value in life. Remember the story of the rich young ruler? "He went away sad because he had great wealth" (Mark 10:17-22).

Immunity

On the hit TV show *Survivor*, 16 people were marooned on a tropical island in the South China Sea to compete against each other for a million-dollar prize. Their goal was to "outwit, outplay, and outlast" each other for 39 days—without getting voted off the island by their fellow castaways. Each week the group met as a tribal council to decide which person would be eliminated from the game and forced to go home empty-handed.

One way to avoid being voted off the island was to achieve immunity. If you had immunity, you were safe—at least, for one tribal council meeting. To get immunity, however, you had to win the week's challenge, a contest that pitted contestants against each other.

One challenge involved eating beetle larvae without squirming. Others involved obstacle courses and endurance events. Every contestant was required to participate in the challenges, but only one could win immunity.

? WHERE TO TAKE IT FROM HERE...

Survivor is an example of reality-based TV. That doesn't necessarily mean the show depicts anything resembling reality; it simply means that the show is relatively unscripted and, therefore, relatively unpredictable.

Obviously, some reality is involved in the concept, which is undoubtedly why the show became so popular. We all know how it feels to be rejected by a group because we aren't good enough, smart enough, attractive enough, or courageous enough. We all know about people who have immunity—those who have accomplished more, accumulated more, or cheated more to get to the top. Our culture's survivor mentality is stressful and discouraging.

Fortunately, you don't have to play *Survivor* to get to heaven. You don't have to outwit, outplay, or outlast anyone to win the prize of eternal life. Though Satan may try vote you off the island, you have nothing to worry about. You have immunity because of what Jesus Christ has done for you on the cross. You don't have to compete for it; all you have to do is accept it.

Jesus won Satan's challenge when he died for the sins of the world and then rose from the dead. When he did that, he won immunity for everyone who would believe in him and trust him as Savior. Do you have immunity?

CAN YOU BE TRUSTED?

Before the breakup of the Soviet Union, Christians were routinely persecuted for their faith by the Communist regime. We have many inspiring stories of courageous Christians behind the Iron Curtain who were willing to die for their faith during this difficult period in world history.

One such story involves a house church in a city in the former Soviet Union. The small group of believers who gathered there were afraid to carry Bibles, so they memorized large sections of the New Testament and recited Scripture to each other.

Each week they would arrive at the house at different times, to avoid arousing the suspicions of KGB informers. On one particular Sunday the church members were all safely inside the building, with the windows closed and doors locked. They began the service by softly singing a hymn and praying.

Suddenly, the door burst open and two soldiers armed with automatic weapons walked in. One shouted, "All right, everybody up against the wall. If you wish to renounce your faith in Jesus Christ, you can leave now and no harm will come to you."

Two or three church members left, then another.

"This is your last chance!" the other soldier warned. "Either turn your back on this Jesus of yours or stay and suffer the consequences!"

Another member left. Two more covered their faces in shame and slipped out into the night. No one else moved. Parents with small children trembling beside them looked down reassuringly. They fully expected to be gunned down on the spot—or, at the very least, imprisoned.

After a few moments of silence, the soldiers closed the door and looked back at the church members left standing against the wall. One of them said, "Keep your hands up—but this time in praise to our Lord Jesus Christ, brothers and sisters. We, too, are Christians. We were sent to another house church several weeks ago to arrest a group of believers. But instead, we were converted."

The other soldier added, "We are sorry to have frightened those who left, but we have learned that unless people are willing to die for their faith, they cannot be fully trusted."

? WHERE TO TAKE IT FROM HERE...

Can you be trusted with the gospel? It is a very precious thing that we have been given—paid for not only by the blood of Jesus, but by the blood of countless martyrs who were willing to die rather than renounce their faith.

We can be thankful that we live in a country where Bibles are plentiful and churches are on every corner, but that doesn't mean we can get by with a shallow, lukewarm faith. The devil is no dummy. He knows that Christianity is only one generation away from being extinct, and he will do all he can to soften us up and make us lazy. Ultimately that will do more harm to the gospel than even our unbelief.

What would you have done when the soldiers arrived? Would you have left or stayed to suffer the consequences? Remember these words of Jesus: "Blessed are you when people insult you, persecute you, and falsely say all kinds of evil against you because of me. Rejoice and be glad, because great is your reward in heaven, for in the same way they persecuted the prophets who were before you" (Matthew 5:11-12).

Dr. Drew's Discovery

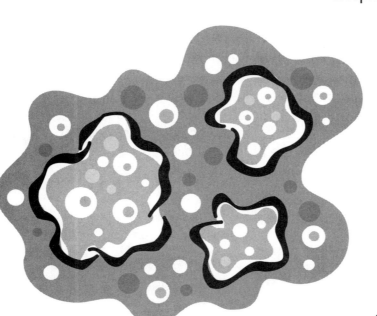

For much of its history, the United States of America has not been so united. For centuries, American society was racially segregated. From schools to buses, public restrooms to drinking fountains, restaurants to churches, the country was divided into black and white.

Hospitals were among the last institutions to desegregate because many people were afraid they might get the "wrong blood" during a transfusion. They feared that if they received blood from a person of another color or ethnicity, they might actually develop the characteristics of that race.

All that changed when Dr. Charles Drew came along.

In the 1930s Dr. Drew created the process we now use to make plasma. Plasma comes from blood, but it is not type-specific, which means it can be used to treat bleeding patients without the need for whole blood.

Dr. Drew's discovery was so noteworthy that he was asked to head the Blood for Britain campaign during World War II. After the war, Drew founded the American Blood Bank, which is still in operation today.

Ironically, Dr. Charles Drew died in 1950 at the age of 46 because he did not receive a blood transfusion or blood plasma in time.

Dr. Drew was injured in an automobile accident and taken to a hospital that was still segregated—a hospital that would not admit black people.

And since Dr. Drew was a black man, he bled to death.

Dr. Charles Drew dedicated his life to saving lives—yet he was unable to save his own.

Sound familiar?

When Jesus was hanging on the cross, the leaders of the religious establishment mocked him. "'He saved others,' they said, 'but he can't save himself! He's the King of Israel! Let him come down now from the cross and we will believe in him!'" (Matthew 27:42).

It is only in retrospect that we can appreciate the injustice of Dr. Drew's death. Because public policy has changed, we may believe we're different from the people of 1950. We cling to the belief that we would have behaved in a more caring manner than those who turned Dr. Drew away during his time of need.

But can we be sure of that?

What about Jesus' death on the cross? Are we any different today than those who mocked the Savior and drove nails through his hands and feet? Unless we truly appreciate what he did for us, we aren't different at all. We have to put our faith in Jesus and make him Lord and Savior of our lives. Only then can we be changed by him from the inside out.

Think of Me

The young man said, "I'm here to help you, ma'am. Why don't you wait in the car where it's warm? By the way, my name is Bryan."

The elderly woman breathed a sigh of relief. There was no way she could have changed her own tire.

Bryan had the spare tire on and the jack down in less than ten minutes. As he was tightening the lug nuts, the woman rolled down her window and began to talk to him. She told him that she was from St. Louis and was only just passing through.

She couldn't thank him enough for coming to her aid. Bryan just smiled as he closed her trunk. She asked him how much she owed him. Any price would have been all right with her. She'd already imagined some of the awful things that might have happened if Bryan hadn't stopped.

Bryan never thought twice about asking for money, even though he could have used some financial help. Changing a tire was not a job to him; it was a matter of helping someone in need.

He told the woman that if she really wanted to pay him back, the next time she saw someone who needed help, she could give that person the assistance they needed. "And when you do," he added, "think of me."

Bryan waited until the woman started her car and drove off. It had been a cold and depressing day, but he felt good as he headed home.

A few miles down the road the woman saw a small diner. Though the place didn't look like much, she went in to grab a bite to eat and take the chill off before she made the last leg of her trip home.

Her waitress brought a clean towel for the woman to dry her wet hair. She had a sweet smile, one that even being on her feet all day couldn't erase. The woman noticed that the waitress was pregnant. She wondered how someone who seemingly had so little could be so generous and kind to a stranger.

Then the woman remembered Bryan. After she finished her meal, she gave the waitress a $100 bill. While the waitress went to get change, the woman slipped quietly out the door.

When the waitress came back to the table, she noticed something written on a napkin. When she picked it up to read it, she noticed four $100 bills that had been left underneath it.

There were tears in the waitress's eyes when she read what the woman had written: "You don't owe me anything. I've been there, too. Somebody nice helped me out, the way I'm helping you. If you really want to pay me back, here is what you do: don't let this chain of love end with you."

That night when the waitress got home from work and climbed into bed, she was thinking about the money and what the woman had written. How could the woman have known how much she and her husband needed that money?

With the baby due in a month, she knew how worried her husband was. As he lay sleeping next to her, she gave him a soft kiss and whispered softly, "Everything's going to be all right. I love you, Bryan."

 WHERE TO TAKE IT FROM HERE...

Jesus said, "Give, and it will be given to you" (Luke 6:38). The unselfish life is the abundant life. God blesses us whenever we are willing to bless others.

Jesus is the supreme example of what it means to be a servant. "Your attitude should be the same as that of Christ Jesus: Who, being in very nature God, did not consider equality with God something to be grasped, but made himself nothing, taking the very nature of a servant...He humbled himself and became obedient to death—even death on a cross!" (Philippians 2:5-8).

And like Bryan in the story, Jesus says to us, "The next time you see someone in need, think of me."

Not Much

With fighter planes flanking its side, the Allied bomber crossed the English Channel, maneuvered its way past German gun turrets, and dropped its load on Berlin. As the convoy started its return flight to England, a group of German fighters appeared on the horizon.

The English and American fighter planes tried to keep the Germans from attacking the bomber, but they were unable to stop every enemy plane. One German fighter made its way through the aerial barrage and managed to get the bomber within its range.

The crew of the bomber watched helplessly as tracer bullets began spitting from the German plane. They stared in horror as five bullets, one after the other, pierced the body of the bomber and penetrated the fuselage, where the gas tanks were located.

Seeing the damage he had inflicted on the bomber's shell, the German fighter pilot turned and headed for home, assuming victory.

The crew of the bomber waited for an explosion or a fire to break out. But nothing happened. Not one spark or puff of smoke appeared. The methodical dripping of gas from the tank was the only evidence of damage to the fuselage.

The bomber managed to land safely at its English airfield. The crew climbed down from the aircraft and carefully removed the shell of the fuselage.

Inside were five nearly perfect bullets. They hadn't exploded; they had merely crumpled. The crew took the bullets back to their barracks for inspection.

When the soldiers opened four of the bullets, they found something amazing. There was no gunpowder inside. They were completely empty.

When they opened the fifth bullet, they found something extraordinary. Rolled into a tiny wad inside the bullet was a note that read:

We are Polish POWs—forced to make bullets in factory. When guards do not look, we do not fill with powder. Is not much, but is best we can do. Please tell family we are alive.

The note was signed by four Polish prisoners of war.

 WHERE TO TAKE IT FROM HERE...

How many times have you been led to believe that what you do for Christ isn't much? How many times have you wondered whether your small efforts, prayers, or attempts to serve make any difference at all?

Don't be misled. Every act of obedience to God is as significant as one of those bullets. Just as one small gesture by a few Polish prisoners saved the life of the crew on that bomber, so one small act of kindness on your part can have a huge impact on someone else's life.

Remember that God uses the small things we do to accomplish big things. He always has. When Jesus wanted to feed several thousand people beside the Sea of Galilee, a little boy came to him with "not much"—just a lunch containing some bread and fish. Jesus said, "Thank you, that will be just fine," and proceeded to feed everyone there.

Don't ever underestimate the power of "not much" when it's in the hands of God.

NEW EARS

Guy Dowd tells this story:

Danny was born with no ears. He could hear all right, but he didn't have ears like normal people. All his life, Danny endured ridicule and rejection because of his deformity. But he learned to live with it. Thankfully, he had loving parents and a strong family to sustain him.

When Danny was in high school, his doctor told him of a new procedure that made it possible to transplant ears from one person to another. That meant Danny could get new ears if someone who was compatible to him ever donated theirs.

This was exciting news. After all, people donated body parts all the time—hearts, lungs, kidneys. But Danny soon found that donor ears were extremely scarce.

Danny didn't give up hope, however. He knew that someday he would get new ears. He graduated from high school with honors and was accepted at a major university thousands of miles away. He kissed his parents good-bye and began his life as a college student. Again, though, he found it hard to make friends and fit in because of his ears.

One day he got a phone call from his father. "Go to the hospital tomorrow, Danny. A donor has been found."

The very next day Danny checked into the university hospital where doctors were ready to perform the surgery. A few hours later, Danny had new ears.

When the bandages came off, Danny gazed into the mirror for hours. He finally had ears like normal people. For the first time in his life, he wasn't ashamed of the way he looked. He not only had new ears, he had a new life.

A few weeks later, Danny received another phone call from his father. "Son, your mother is very ill," his father said. "She may not live through the night."

Danny was on the first plane home. When he arrived, his father

gave him the sad news that his mother had died.

Together they went to the funeral home, where Danny was able to see his mother for the last time. He leaned over to kiss her cheek. Brushing her hair back from her face, he noticed that she had no ears.

? WHERE TO TAKE IT FROM HERE...

It was a mother's incredible love that provided Danny with new ears. And it was a Father's incredible love that provided us with new life. "But God demonstrates his own love for us in this: While we were still sinners, Christ died for us" (Romans 5:8).

Dancing in a Toll Booth

Tim Timmons shares this:

If you've ever gone through a toll booth, you know that your relationship to the person in the booth is not the most intimate you'll ever have. It's one of life's frequent nonencounters. You hand over some money; you might get change; you drive off. I've been through every one of the 17 toll booths on the Oakland-San Francisco Bay Bridge on thousands of occasions and never had an exchange worth remembering with anybody.

Late one morning in 1984, headed for lunch in San Francisco, I drove toward one of the booths. I heard loud music. It sounded

like a party or a Michael Jackson concert. I looked around. No other cars with their windows open. No sound trucks. I looked at the toll booth. Inside it, the man was dancing.

"What are you doing?" I asked.

"I'm having a party," he said.

"What about the rest of these people?" I looked over at other booths; nothing moving there. "They're not invited."

I had a dozen other questions for him, but somebody in a big hurry to get somewhere started punching his horn behind me, and I drove off. But I made a note to myself: find this guy again. Something in his eye says there's magic in his toll booth.

Months later I did find him again, still with the loud music, still having a party. Again I asked, "What are you doing?"

He said, "I remember you from the last time. I'm still dancing. I'm having the same party."

I said, "Look. What about the rest of the people?"

He said. "Stop. What do those look like to you?" He pointed down the row of toll booths.

"They look like...toll booths," I said.

"Nooooo imagination!"

"Okay, I give up. What do they look like to you?"

He said, "Vertical coffins."

"What are you talking about?"

"I can prove it. At 8:30 every morning, live people get in. Then they die for eight hours. At 4:30, like Lazarus from the dead, they reemerge and go home. For eight hours, their brains are on hold, dead on the job. Going through the motions."

I was amazed. This guy had developed a philosophy, a mythology about his job. I couldn't help asking the next question: "Why is it different for you? You're having a good time."

He looked at me. "I knew you were going to ask that," he paused. "I'm going to be a dancer someday." He pointed to the administration building. "My bosses are in there, and they're paying for my training."

Sixteen people dead on the job, and the 17th—in precisely the same environment—figures out a way to live. That man was having a party where you and I probably wouldn't last three days.

He and I had lunch later, and he said, "I don't understand why anybody would think my job is boring. I have a corner office, glass on all sides. I can see the Golden Gate, San Francisco, the Berkeley hills. Half of the Western world comes here on vacation. And I just stroll in every day and practice dancing."

(?) WHERE TO TAKE IT FROM HERE...

Every day you have a choice. You can choose a vertical coffin or a dance studio. It's all up to you. "This day...I have set before you life and death, blessings and curses. Now choose life, so that you and your children may live!" (Deuteronomy 30:19).

The Missing Dollar

Here's a little arithmetic problem for you:

Three brothers check into a hotel and rent one room. The hotel clerk informs them that the room is $30 for the night, so each brother chips in $10 and they pay for the room in advance.

About an hour later, the clerk discovers that he charged the brothers the weekend rate of $30 instead of the weekday rate of $25. He gives the bellhop five $1 bills to return to the brothers. On the way up to the room, the bellhop realizes that five dollars can't be divided evenly among three brothers, so he only refunds them $3 and pockets the other $2.

Each brother originally paid $10 for his share of the $30 room and received a $1 refund from the bellhop. That means they ended up each spending $9 ($10 minus $1) on the room—or $27 ($9 times 3). Add in the $2 the bellhop kept for a total of $29.

What happened to the extra dollar, and who lost what?

Here's the answer:

The extra dollar isn't lost. After the bellhop refunded $1 to each brother, they ended up paying a total of $27 for the room ($9 each). The hotel received $25 after it refunded the $5 the bellhop was supposed to deliver. The bellhop pocketed $2 of the brothers' money. Add his $2 to the $25 the hotel received, and you get $27, the same amount that was paid by the three brothers. In other words, the money out—what the brothers paid—equals the money in—what both the hotel and bellhop received.

What makes this problem confusing is the way it's explained. The dollar seems to disappear when adding part of what was received (the $2 kept by the bellhop) to what was paid ($27). That's adding apples and oranges—and guarantees a wrong result.

And who lost what? The bellhop lost his job when the three brothers stopped by the front desk to thank the clerk for sending up their $3 refund!

? WHERE TO TAKE IT FROM HERE...

If you're still confused about the arithmetic, don't worry. Unless you're planning to become an accountant, it's okay to be confused. It's not okay, however, to be confused about the behavior of the bellhop.

Unfortunately, many people today are very confused about issues of right and wrong. We live in a society that has made ethics a matter of personal preference. Surveys show that a majority of youth see nothing wrong with cheating on exams, and a majority of adults see nothing wrong with cheating on income taxes. Today's young people are sometimes called the whatever generation because they suffer from a lack of moral and ethical guidance.

But Christians shouldn't have any confusion about such matters. We have the Word of God to guide us and to inform our moral and ethical decision-making. Contrary to the world's way of thinking, right and wrong is not something that you decide. All you have to decide is whether you're willing to obey.

"Anyone, then, who knows the good he ought to do and doesn't do it, sins" (James 4:17).

The Love Life of the Frog

A congressman once publicly criticized the Department of Agriculture for wasting the taxpayers' money printing useless pamphlets. According to the congressman, they printed pamphlets about "everything except the love life of the frog."

Following the congressman's speech, the Department of Agriculture began to receive orders for *The Love Life of the Frog.* As more and more orders arrived, the department eventually had to make a public statement announcing emphatically that no such pamphlet existed.

After the public denial, letters requesting *The Love Life of the Frog* began to arrive by the hundreds. Finally, the Secretary of Agriculture, in a national address, stated that the department had never printed such a pamphlet and had no intention of ever doing so.

Following the broadcast, thousands of orders for the pamphlet arrived in the mail.

 WHERE TO TAKE IT FROM HERE...

When a company approaches an advertising firm about marketing its product, one of the first things the advertising folks tell them is to get the name of the product in front of the consumers. Name recognition is usually the single best indicator of the number of consumers who will purchase a product. This is true even in the political arena—people tend to vote for someone whose name they recognize, even when they're ignorant of the candidate's position on important political issues.

Just because you hear a statement over and over again doesn't make it true. Those looking for truth need to look to Jesus. "I am the way and the truth, and the life." (John 14:6)

184

Uncovering the Art

ichelangelo is considered one of the greatest Renaissance painters and sculptors.

In talking about his sculpting, he said that he never created his great works; he discovered them. He said he uncovered them.

Using his famous statue of David as an example, he said God placed the art in the stone, and it was Michelangelo's job to bring out what God had created. Trying to see what was waiting to be uncovered, he was known to stand in front of an unfinished piece and yell in frustration, "Come out!"

? WHERE TO TAKE IT FROM HERE...

As children of God, we're called to live lives of purity and holiness. Many of us, though, try to be good under our own power. God is more than powerful enough—and more than willing—to make us into who we were originally created to be. Our job, then, is to allow God to chip away all of the parts of us that don't belong. When we allow these extras to be trimmed off by the Master's hand, we'll find beautiful works of art—glorious creations made in the image and likeness of God. "[I am] confident of this, that he who began a good work in you will carry it on to completion until the day of Christ Jesus." (Philippians 1:6).

Columbus's Legacy

For hundreds of years before Christopher Columbus was born, the motto of Spain was *ne plus ultra*. This is Latin for "no more beyond." You see, the Spaniards believed that they'd already discovered everything worth discovering.

One of the most beautiful monuments to Christopher Columbus today is a statue in Spain of a huge lion with the words *ne plus ultra* underneath. However, the lion is eating the first word *ne*. All that can be read is "more beyond." This was Columbus's greatest legacy—he proved that there was more beyond.

(?) WHERE TO TAKE IT FROM HERE...

Jesus, too, has shown us that there is more beyond. Like the Columbus monument's lion eating the words, the Lion of Judah erased the notion that death was the end. Through Christ's death on the cross and resurrection from the dead, we can all say with assurance that there is plus ultra—*more beyond! "Death has been swallowed up in victory. Where, O death, is your victory? Where, O death, is your sting? The sting of death is sin, and the power of sin is the law. But thanks be to God! He gives us the victory through our Lord Jesus Christ" (1 Corinthians 15:54-57).*

Wrong Order!

How do you respond when a mistake has been made with your fast-food order? If you're 6'3" and weigh 270 pounds, people don't recommend crawling through the drive-through window.

But that's exactly what happened when a University of Kansas football player realized a chalupa was left out of his Taco Bell order. He got so angry that he tried to climb through the 14- by 46-inch drive-through window and got stuck.

The frightened manager and employees locked themselves in an office and called the police.

The police pulled up to the drive-through and laughed hysterically as they discovered the legs and back end of the football player kicking in midair. Police Sergeant George Wheeler said, "When you take a big guy and put him through a small space, something's got to give."

? WHERE TO TAKE IT FROM HERE...

Wow! What an outrageous thing to do...or is it? Maybe you've done something out of anger that was just as foolish and just as ridiculous as jumping through a fast-food window? Our actions are often just as silly—though perhaps more ordinary—when we get angry: intentionally cutting down a person in front of others, getting into a fistfight, starting a mean rumor (whether true or untrue), giving someone the silent treatment.

Though these are very natural human responses, Paul warns that this is not the way God wants us to act. "Get rid of all bitterness, rage and anger, brawling and slander, along with every form of malice. Be kind and compassionate to one another, forgiving each other, just as in Christ God forgave you" (Ephesians 4:31-32).

Amy Carmichael

As a young Irishwoman working in England in the late 1800s, Amy Carmichael decided to answer God's call to serve in the mission field. Twice rejected for medical reasons, she eventually found a mission agency willing to put her on a ship and send her to India. She arrived with a tropical fever and a temperature of 105. Some missionaries who met her believed she wouldn't last six months. But Amy recovered, and she never went home.

The young missionary soon discovered that the way to reach the Indian people was not through preaching but through sacrifice. She wrote, "If the ultimate, the hardest, cannot be asked of me, if my fellows hesitate to ask it and turn to someone else, then I know nothing of Calvary love."

So she reached out to the poorest, youngest, and most despised among them, especially the babies and children given to the Hindu temples who were forced to serve as slaves and were tortured if they were caught trying to escape. She said, "There were days when the sky turned black for me because of what I heard and knew was true. Sometimes it was as if I saw the Lord Jesus Christ kneeling alone, as he knelt long ago under the olive trees. And the only thing that one who cared could do was to go softly and kneel down beside him, so that he would not be alone in his sorrow over the little children."

Amy not only felt sorrow for the children, but she was spurred to action. She rescued them, built a home, and recruited a staff to care for them. The ministry became known as Dohnavur Fellowship, and the children called its headmistress *Amma*—the Tamil word for mother. To those who profited from the enslavement practices, she was known as "the white woman who steals children."

Amy Carmichael's mission trip ended 55 years later, when she died at the age of 83. During that time she rescued over 1,000 abused, abandoned, and enslaved children. And though her stories, prayers, and devotions filled 35 books back in Britain, not once did she return to hear the praises of her friends and supporters. To Amy anything that called attention to herself stole attention from the God she served. In fact in 1919, her name was published in a British honors list. When she found out about it, she wrote back to England asking to have her name removed. It troubled her to "have an experience so different from his who was despised and rejected—not kindly honored."

Ironically, the woman who wanted no honor other than that of being Christ's servant became famous nonetheless, as tens of thousands of readers in Britain and America were moved by her writings. Her example of sacrificial love has encouraged countless numbers of Christians to follow her into the mission field.

? WHERE TO TAKE IT FROM HERE...

Many around the world are crying out right now against injustice, poverty, and prejudice. As God's children we are called to carry each another's burdens (Galatians 6:2). Jesus himself told us that when we care for "the least of these," we do it for him (Matthew 25:31-46).

Contributors

Glenn Ansley, Jr.
Holy Bucket!

Dan Bergstrom
Baboons on the Loose

Jeff Bordon
Bad Tire, Good Business
Do You Know Me?
Dr. Drew's Discovery
The Love Life of a Frog
Not Much
Ramu

Rick Bundschuh
The Egg Toss
It's the Water
On the Right Track
Only a Prayer
Shake It Off
Sobibor
They Said Yes

Steve Case
The Choice
Do Something!
Soaring
Stepping

Les Christie
Giving It Up For a Friend
That's My Child

Pat Croash
The Bus Driver's Gift
Farmer Flemming

Nick Davis
E-Flat

Guy Doud
New Ears

Andrew Emery
Jason's Worst Christmas

Gregg Farah
Wrong Order!

Greg Griffin
Real Pearls

Bobby Howard
Pull, Buddy!

**John D. King
(Padre Juan King)**
The House in the Dark

Dan Knuff
An Altitude Problem

Michael Kohl
A Great Man

Tic Long
Uncovering the Art

J.D. McCarty
The Dirty Dollar

Scott Meier
The Parable of the Baseball Team

Tony Myles
Think of Me

Darrell Pearson
The CPR Class
Early Flubber
Who's Watching?

Marv Penner
Giving It Up For a Friend

Kara Powell
Alyssa
Bored and Busy
The List
Not a Good Example

James Prior
Columbus's Legacy
Through Thick and Thin

Mark Riddle
Hep Baddy

Sonny Salsbury
Bobby's Valentines

Todd Temple
Amy Carmichael

Tim Timmons
Dancing in a Toll Booth

Chuck Workman
The Giant
Lashed to the Mast
Saved by Stirrups

Chuck Wysong
Can You Be Trusted?

The author and publisher acknowledge that some of the stories in this volume are of unknown origin, having been circulated orally or electronically, and without bylines or other identifying information. We've made every effort to track down the source of every story in this book. We apologize for any omissions.

Resources from Youth Specialties

Youth Ministry Programming

Camps, Retreats, Missions, & Service Ideas (Ideas Library)
Compassionate Kids: Practical Ways to Involve Your Students in Mission and Service
Creative Bible Lessons from the Old Testament
Creative Bible Lessons in 1 & 2 Corinthians
Creative Bible Lessons in Galatians and Philippians
Creative Bible Lessons in John: Encounters with Jesus
Creative Bible Lessons in Romans: Faith on Fire!
Creative Bible Lessons on the Life of Christ
Creative Bible Lessons in Psalms
Creative Junior High Programs from A to Z, Vol. 1 (A-M)
Creative Junior High Programs from A to Z, Vol. 2 (N-Z)
Creative Meetings, Bible Lessons, & Worship Ideas (Ideas Library)
Crowd Breakers & Mixers (Ideas Library)
Downloading the Bible Leader's Guide
Drama, Skits, & Sketches (Ideas Library)
Drama, Skits, & Sketches 2 (Ideas Library)
Drama, Skits, & Sketches 3 (Ideas Library)
Dramatic Pauses
Everyday Object Lessons
Games (Ideas Library)
Games 2 (Ideas Library)
Games 3 (Ideas Library)
Good Sex: A Whole-Person Approach to Teenage Sexuality & God
Great Fundraising Ideas for Youth Groups
More Great Fundraising Ideas for Youth Groups
Great Retreats for Youth Groups
Holiday Ideas (Ideas Library)
Hot Illustrations CD-ROM
Hot Illustrations for Youth Talks
Hot Illustrations for Youth Talks 4
More Hot Illustrations for Youth Talks
Still More Hot Illustrations for Youth Talks
Ideas Library on CD-ROM
Incredible Questionnaires for Youth Ministry
Junior High Game Nights
More Junior High Game Nights
Kickstarters: 101 Ingenious Intros to Just about Any Bible Lesson
Live the Life! Student Evangelism Training Kit
Memory Makers
The Next Level Leader's Guide
Play It! Over 150 Great Games for Youth Groups
Roaring Lambs
Screen Play
So What Am I Gonna Do With My Life?
Special Events (Ideas Library)
Spontaneous Melodramas
Spontaneous Melodramas 2
Student Leadership Training Manual
Student Underground: An Event Curriculum on the Persecuted Church
Super Sketches for Youth Ministry

Talking the Walk
Teaching the Bible Creatively
Videos That Teach
What Would Jesus Do? Youth Leader's Kit
Wild Truth Bible Lessons
Wild Truth Bible Lessons 2
Wild Truth Bible Lessons—Pictures of God
Worship Services for Youth Groups

Professional Resources

Administration, Publicity, & Fundraising (Ideas Library)
Dynamic Communicators Workshop
Equipped to Serve: Volunteer Youth Worker Training Course
Great Talk Outlines for Youth Ministry
Help! I'm a Junior High Youth Worker!
Help! I'm a Small-Group Leader!
Help! I'm a Sunday School Teacher!
Help! I'm an Urban Youth Worker!
Help! I'm a Volunteer Youth Worker!
How to Expand Your Youth Ministry
How to Speak to Youth...and Keep Them Awake at the Same Time
Junior High Ministry (Updated & Expanded)
The Ministry of Nurture: A Youth Worker's Guide to Discipling Teenagers
Postmodern Youth Ministry
Purpose-Driven® Youth Ministry
Purpose-Driven® Youth Ministry Training Kit
So That's Why I Keep Doing This! 52 Devotional Stories for Youth Workers
A Youth Ministry Crash Course
Youth Ministry Management Tools
The Youth Worker's Handbook to Family Ministry

Academic Resources

Four Views of Youth Ministry & the Church
Starting Right: Thinking Theologically About Youth Ministry
Youth Ministry That Transforms

Discussion Starters

Discussion & Lesson Starters (Ideas Library)
Discussion & Lesson Starters 2 (Ideas Library)
EdgeTV
Get 'Em Talking
Keep 'Em Talking!
Good Sex: A Whole-Person Approach to Teenage Sexuality & God
High School TalkSheets—Updated!
More High School TalkSheets—Updated!
High School TalkSheets from Psalms and Proverbs—Updated!
Junior High-Middle School TalkSheets—Updated!
More Junior High-Middle School TalkSheets—Updated!
Junior High-Middle School TalkSheets from Psalms and Proverbs—Updated!
Real Kids: Short Cuts
Real Kids: The Real Deal—on Friendship, Loneliness, Racism, & Suicide
Real Kids: The Real Deal—on Sexual Choices, Family Matters, & Loss

Real Kids: The Real Deal—on Stressing Out, Addictive Behavior, Great Comebacks, & Violence
Real Kids: Word on the Street
Unfinished Sentences: 450 Tantalizing Statement-Starters to Get Teenagers Talking & Thinking
What If...? 450 Thought-Provoking Questions to Get Teenagers Talking, Laughing, and Thinking
Would You Rather...? 465 Provocative Questions to Get Teenagers Talking
Have You Ever...? 450 Intriguing Questions Guaranteed to Get Teenagers Talking

Art Source Clip Art

Stark Raving Clip Art (print)
Youth Group Activities (print)
Clip Art Library Version 2.0 (CD-ROM)

Digital Resources

Clip Art Library Version 2.0 (CD-ROM)
Hot Illustrations CD-ROM
Ideas Library on CD-ROM
Great Talk Outlines for Youth Ministry
Screen Play
Youth Ministry Management Tools

Videos & Video Curricula

Dynamic Communicators Workshop
EdgeTV
Equipped to Serve: Volunteer Youth Worker Training Course
The Heart of Youth Ministry: A Morning with Mike Yaconelli
Live the Life! Student Evangelism Training Kit
Purpose-Driven® Youth Ministry Training Kit
Real Kids: Short Cuts
Real Kids: The Real Deal—on Friendship, Loneliness, Racism, & Suicide
Real Kids: The Real Deal—on Sexual Choices, Family Matters, & Loss
Real Kids: The Real Deal—on Stressing Out, Addictive Behavior, Great Comebacks, & Violence
Real Kids: Word on the Street
Student Underground: An Event Curriculum on the Persecuted Church
Understanding Your Teenager Video Curriculum
Youth Ministry Outside the Lines

Student Resources

Downloading the Bible: A Rough Guide to the New Testament
Downloading the Bible: A Rough Guide to the Old Testament
Grow For It Journal through the Scriptures
So What Am I Gonna Do With My Life?
Spiritual Challenge Journal: The Next Level
Teen Devotional Bible
What (Almost) Nobody Will Tell You about Sex
What Would Jesus Do? Spiritual Challenge Journal
Wild Truth Journal for Junior Highers
Wild Truth Journal—Pictures of God
Wild Truth Journal—Pictures of God 2